Contents

UNFUCK YOUR COMMUNICATION

Using Science to Connect, Collaborate, and Make Yourself Heard

Dr. Faith G. Harper, ACS, ACN

Microcosm Publishing

Portland, Ore | Cleveland, Ohio

UNFUCK YOUR COMMUNICATION: Using Science to Connect, Collaborate, and Make Yourself Heard

© Dr. Faith G. Harper, 2025

First edition - 3,000 copies - July 1, 2025

ISBN 9781648412660
This is Microcosm # 976

Edited by Lex Orgera
Cover and design by Joe Biel
This edition © Microcosm Publishing, 2025
For a catalog, write or visit:
Microcosm Publishing
2752 N Williams Ave.
Portland, OR 97227

www.Microcosm.Pub

All the news that's fit to print at www.Microcosm.Pub/Newsletter
Find more Dr. Faith titles at www.Microcosm.Pub/DrFaith

Get more copies of this book at *www.Microcosm.Pub/Communication*
**To join the ranks of high-class stores that feature Microcosm titles, talk
to your rep:** In the U.S. **COMO** (Atlantic), **ABRAHAM** (Midwest),
BOB BARNETT (Texas, Arkansas, Oklahoma, Louisiana),
IMPRINT (Pacific), **TURNAROUND** (Europe), **UTP/MANDA**
(Canada), **NEWSOUTH** (Australia/New Zealand), **Observatoire**
(Africa, Europe), **IPR** (Middle East), **Yvonne Chau** (Southeast
Asia), **HarperCollins** (India), **Everest/B.K. Agency** (China),
Tim Burland (Japan/Korea), , or **FAIRE** in the gift trade.

Did you know that you can buy our books directly from us at sliding
scale rates? Support a small, independent publisher and pay less than
Amazon's price at **www.Microcosm.Pub**.

Global labor conditions are bad, and our roots in industrial Cleveland in the
'70s and '80s made us appreciate the need to treat workers right. Therefore,
our books are MADE IN THE USA.

EU Safety Information: https://microcosmpublishing.com/gpsr

MICROCOSM·PUBLISHING

Microcosm Publishing is Portland's most diversified publishing house and distributor, with a focus on the colorful, authentic, and empowering. Our books and zines have put your power in your hands since 1996, equipping readers to make positive changes in their lives and in the world around them. Microcosm emphasizes skill-building, showing hidden histories, and fostering creativity through challenging conventional publishing wisdom with books and bookettes about DIY skills, food, bicycling, gender, self-care, and social justice. What was once a distro and record label started by Joe Biel in a drafty bedroom was determined to be *Publishers Weekly*'s fastest-growing publisher of 2022 and #3 in 2023, and is now among the oldest independent publishing houses in Portland, OR, and Cleveland, OH. We are a politically moderate, centrist publisher in a world that has inched to the right for the past 80 years.

INTRODUCTION

*C*ommunication is a skill that isn't really taught, ennit? I mean, it wasn't until I was in graduate school for a degree that was foundationally supported by communication (you know, being a mental health professional) that I got any real coursework on how we share with others, both verbally and nonverbally, and how to attend to what they share with us.

And honestly, learning about communication was the hardest part of therapist training for me and most therapists I know.

No one likes to think they suck at communication. We know what we mean, right? But when we say it, sometimes others think we mean something completely different. And why is that? Because communication is based on a shared understanding, which means there are nearly 8 billion ways of understanding the world.

That whole bridging your worldview to someone else's? So you can make sure your intent is clear? This shit is hard.

In the 90s (yes, last century, I am an old person), we had a significant communication failure in community mental health that served as a warning to us all. There is a pre–industrialized society treatment for ear infections that is referred to as "fuego." Which, yes, means fire. A piece of wax-coated paper is rolled up tightly and put into the ear canal, and then the paper is set on fire. The idea is to create a vacuum that helps pull out earwax, fluid buildup, bacteria, etc. Which promotes healing and mitigates the pain of an ear infection.

In this particular instance, a child had an ear infection, and her mama went to fuego her ear. Now, paper without the wax dip burns faster, so you use a much larger sheet of paper. Mom couldn't find one big enough, so she pulled a sheet out of the phone book.[1] If you are a fellow old person who remembers the type of paper used in phone books, you know exactly what happened. The page incinerated immediately, causing some light burns to the daughter's face.

Mom immediately brought her to the ER and was working to explain, in Spanish, what had happened. She used the colloquial expression that she was looking to get the demons out of her daughter's ear. Again, this is the common expression used to define the practice and doesn't mean that anyone thought there were ear canal demons. (It's no different from me using a common Indigenous expression to compliment someone's fit: me telling you that you look deadly means you look fantastic. But if you don't know that expression you may take it some-kinda-way, right?)

And you can guess what happened next, right? ER staff were worried this lady had a thought

1 Back in the Wild West of the 1900s, our phones were on the walls of our homes. Not carried in our pockets. And the numbers for everyone, including businesses, were printed in a book the phone company gave you every year. (Cuz you couldn't just look them up on the then-nascent internet.) This phone book also had pizza coupons in it, so it was quite useful.

disorder or some kind of psychotic break and she was held at the psych unit of the same-said hospital.

For several days.

Until someone who actually knew the cultural context of the expression interviewed her and threw down until she got released.

And you may be thinking . . . ok, Doc . . . but that was a minute ago. That isn't a problem anymore right? We all get DEI training. (At least in the states that haven't outlawed it yet.) It isn't still this bad-bad.

Except it is.

Take this other story from a situation I was directly involved in less than a decade ago. One of the certified family partners (CFPs) in my organization came to me to staff a case: a mom and son who were both diagnosed with schizophrenia and were receiving community mental health services. There is definitely a genetic component to thought disorders, so that's not unheard of.

The son was eight years old. Having a thought disorder diagnosis that young is rare, but again not unheard of. As the keeper of those statistics at that time, I can tell you he was one of three prepubescent kids in the county with that diagnosis when this issue was unfolding.

Another thing that made this case unusual was that the mom and son seemed to be experiencing the same delusion, a phenomenon then called a folie à deux (now currently listed in the DSM as "shared delusional disorder" or "induced delusional disorder" in the ICD). Meaning the mom and son were experiencing the exact same delusion. Also very rare, but not unheard of. I had seen that once before in my career.

However, with these two individuals, the shared delusion was one of seeing a ghost in the home.

But now we have three very rare things stacked together. And the CFP was curious if they were missing something. Upon chatting with the mom, she realized that the family was Indigenous. Not "just" Mexican-American. Of course, most everyone with Mexican heritage is Indigenous, but many have lost their cultural roots due to colonization, and may not even know the name of their original nation. This particular family had held these traditions and practiced them. So the CFP (hi Patti!) came to me and asked if there was something that the care team might be missing that they should consider.

I suggested that the CFP ask the mom if they were ghost sick.

"Ghost sickness" is a common grief expression seen with many Indigenous peoples, not just of Turtle Island (the Americas) but also of the Polynesian Islands, East Asia, and Southeast Asia. The idea is that these spirits visit the bereaved, especially if their loved one's death was not a peaceful one. It is one of the most common culture-bound syndromes clinicians will see.

And, yes. Mom endorsed ghost sickness brought on by the passing of a beloved uncle. We smudged and salt-sealed their home and assisted in ceremony to encourage the spirit of the uncle to find peace and move on.

And their shared delusion was cured. Both ended up released from services.

I shared this story in *Understanding Indigenous Perspectives* as a caution around understanding culture when providing diagnosis and care. However, first and foremost, this example is a story about communication. About the breakdowns that lie within it. And it's a reminder that you don't have to know all the things to be a good communicator. Patti the CFP didn't. But she knew what she didn't know and found someone who had a better chance of knowing and she asked. And she then used the information she learned to facilitate the care that the clients actually needed.

And the power differential in these cases made the consequences much easier to track, so the responsibility for the breakdowns is much easier to assign. But all missed communication has consequences. And the consequences could be just as severe.

I've seen it in real time when working with couples and families in sessions. Where one person said something to the other that was received poorly. I knew what they meant, but it wasn't what they said. And the person they said it to (their partner, their kiddo, whoever) was understandably upset and activated.

The fights, and flights, and freezes—and all the other relationship breakdowns—start to make sense. Because we rarely have someone else in the room that can say, "Hold up, you said XYZ. Did you mean exactly XYZ? Or did you mean ABC or DEF?"

Because almost never does the person in question say, "Yup, I meant to say something shitty and attacking. Gimme a megaphone and I'll say it the fuck again."

Instead, generally, people are horrified, self-correct, and recognize that the missed meanings in their communication are a bigger problem than the problem itself. And then we know what to work on for the future health of their relationships.

But communication isn't just for communicating with your partner and family members. It's everyone, everywhere. We can call communication a soft skill in the business world, but it is an indispensable one. Communicating effectively with our friends, our acquaintances, and everyone we interact with in public spaces makes life so much more livable—when we can keep the problem contained to what it is, rather than adding our communication misfires to the mess that is modern life.

So at this point, maybe you are recognizing conversations you've heard about, witnessed, or participated in as being way bigger than they needed to be because of communication misfires. And I hope you are also seeing that this book is for literally everyone. Because we all communicate. And we all could do much, much better at it.

All of my other books land on communication strategies at some point, because we live in community and have to work through the issues that my books address with the people who are in our communities. For this reason, I am a big believer in having scripts. That is, plans for how you are going to address an issue so you can be skillfully proactive instead of ratchetly reactive. In the pages to come, these strategies are all compiled here with a bunch more research-y info to help you better understand the "ok, but why" of these skills.

(There's also a companion workbook for my peeps who are very workbookish. If you want the skills extracted from the researchy-y parts, there they are. With space for doing your own self-communication on paper and the like. But the book makes sense just fine without the workbook. And vice-versa. Because I hate sneaky in-app purchases like that.)

Still with me? Let's chat.

Grounding Exercise: The Reorientation Countdown

Firstly (or, ok, secondly) I want to offer you a good grounding exercise you can use if reading this book brings up any issues that are emotionally expensive for you. When we get activated, we get immersed in the situation we are thinking about, past or present, rather than aware of our immediate surroundings. This grounding skill brings your focus back on the present—reorienting you to the world around you, instead of what your brain started focusing on internally. It's super simple, but what makes it work is you have to look outward instead of inward. It's also referred to as the 5-4-3-2-1 sense game. Because what you are going to do is:

Notice

- 5 things you can see

- 4 things you can hear

- 3 things you can smell

- 2 things you can touch

- 1 thing you can taste

By focusing on your immediate and present circumstances, it becomes easier to keep yourself in your thinking brain, with all the accompanying executive function skills we like to keep on hand.

WHAT MAKES UP OUR COMMUNICATION

What Is Communication?

T he word communication comes from the Latin *communicare*, meaning "to share." That's it. That's the whole thing. We communicate to share information, our lives, experiences, wants, needs, cute panda bear videos, etc. So communication is the process through which we, verbally and nonverbally, share messages with others. Hopefully successfully!

Though, of course, if we were naturally successful at this sharing, there would be no need to write books about it.

Types of Communication

Generally, the experts divide communication into four different types. However, Dr. Anne Converse

Willkomm, a Drexel University professor who teaches a Communications for Professionals course, advocates for five. I happen to agree with her, (which clearly means she is objectively correct), so I'm sharing this list as five.

Verbal communication is the part most of us think of first. It is the use of our voice to make noises that theoretically convey a shared meaning to the people who hear what we say. It's the words we say and it's how we say them (cadence, pitch, tone, etc.). Don't discount the "how" part. A client recently told me that I was telling her the exact same thing her neurologist was telling her, but I used a tone of voice that was more curious, and possibility-based, and explorative, rather than bossy and determined to sway her will. She told me that my tone made it clear that it was her decision, so she was more open to it, instead of cranky and dismissive because some dude was bossing her around. And as Dr. Wilkomm points out, if we can see the other person's body while they are talking (in person, video, etc.), the verbal cannot be divorced from the nonverbal. In the case above, in addition to the tone I used, I was sitting with the client with open body language, a shrug of my shoulders, and other indicators of "I dunno what's right for you babe, you know yourself better than I do, but it might make sense for these reasons?" All these things reinforced that I was encouraging openness to possibilities, not trying to sway her decision.

Nonverbal communication is the mostly noiseless ways we use our body to share information with others. Our posture. How we use our fingers, hands, and arms to punctuate. Our facial expressions. Our eye contact. Other eye movements (eye rolling, side-eye, etc). Our space between our body and the body of others when we are physically in the same space. Any touch we employ when physically in the same space. We may also make noises that aren't words. Like sighing. Or snapping our tongues on the roofs of our mouths. Or humming. Stuff like that. So nonverbal communication might look like someone saying, "Yeah, it's all good." And maybe their tone of voice is congruent with that. As in, it doesn't sound sarcastic or anything equally obvious. But then their body language is tight and their arms are folded across their body protectively or they aren't making the level of eye contact that is typical for them, etc.

Written communication is words put somewhere for someone else's eyes to reach them. If you are reading this book on slices of dead tree or on the screen of a device, it's written communication. If it's an audiobook, then we're back to verbal, right? Written communication is meant to have the same purpose as verbal communication. A clear sharing of information. But written communication isn't a natural skill everyone has. And honestly? As a recovering academic, I think most professional writing is almost an entirely different language. A dense one designed to demonstrate how smart we are, rather than designed to share information clearly. It's not helpful to make people slog through your great idea. I prefer writing that sounds like a verbal conversation in my head. I've also found that neurospicy peeps fare much, much better in consuming written communication when the writing feels like the flow of verbal communication.

Visual communication is made up of the photos, videos, and other images that share messages. Visual communication may have verbal, nonverbal, and written elements, but it tends to have a more holistic message to share, and often a very emotional one. For example, a photo of a sunset or a video of a kitten making biscuits—things like these share tons of information . . . and can draw us in without any words written or said.

And listening is the vital fifth type of communication—because every other style relies on it. Receiving what others are sharing and trying to understand what they are working to convey is the entire point of all of it. We share information for it to be received. Listening is the act of receiving. Even in volatile situations, we can't progress or even de-escalate without hearing what others are saying.

Within the above types of communication, we have communication styles. We can display any of these styles within any of the types of communication, so that's what we'll turn our attention to next.

Styles of Communication

The following styles are ways you might find yourself communicating in different situations and with different people.

AGGRESSIVE An aggressive communication style tends to be excessively harsh. Aggressive communicators tend to interrupt others, disregard others' opinions, and continually reinforce their own worldview and "rightness." Have you ever met anyone like this? Seen a politician on TV act like this? You know the type. If you admit you are waiting for pumpkin spice latte season to start, they roll their eyes and tell you that's bougie and dumb, your taste is shitty, and you need to stop. The meta-message of aggressive communicators is "I'm cool and you're a dumbass."

A passive communication style tends to be ineffective in helping people protect themselves and hold their center. Passive communicators often don't make their wants and needs known, and say that things are fine when

PASSIVE

they are really, totally, deeply not fine. Passive communicators tend to defer to others, praising them while dumping on themselves. This isn't the same thing as letting someone you know and trust help guide you to better decision-making in a crisis. This is about never feeling like you can authentically advocate for what is right for you. Passive communicators might say "Oh, pumpkin spice lattes! Let's get those. I mean, I'm lactose intolerant and I'm gonna get really sick, but I can deal. It's totally ok." The meta-message of passive communicators is "I'm a hot mess, but you're totally cool, so you make the decisions for both of us."

An assertive communication style is our sweet spot in most cases (unless your literal safety is on the line and being situationally aggressive

ASSERTIVE

or passive makes sense). Assertive communicators are firm in their belief systems and speak in a way that is congruent with their actions but still respects differing viewpoints. Back to the PSL example I apparently cannot let go of: if you say you want your pumpkin spice latte, they may respond with "Glad to see you out there living your best life, loving what you love. Could you order me an iced americano, though? That's more my jam." The meta-message of assertive communicators is "I'm cool and you're totally cool too. Even if we don't agree."

Some questions to reflect on:

- What is your communication style most of the time? Is it different in different circumstances or with different people?

- What messages have you internalized about your right to healthy communication and ownership of your values and beliefs?

- If you communicate differently in certain situations, or with certain people, what about those relationships causes you to change?

- How close is your current communication style to what your ideal balance would be?

- What is the first place you can start to shift your communication style, moving closer to your ideal? How will you go about doing that?

If you don't communicate as well as you would like to, owning that is really important.

As in, "Hey friend! I realized recently that I don't communicate things that are important to me nearly as well as I should. Like the other night when I agreed to meet you for coffee but then didn't drink mine and complained the whole time and you ended up confused AF, which is understandable. I'm working on that. So what I've been trying to say, albeit, not well, is, next time we hang out can we go for a walk instead? Or something else without the temptation of delicious coffee drinks that make me sick but I still can't resist them?"

If you have this conversation, I'm totally awarding you a gold star for badass adulting.

The biggest thing to remember here is that it is a process. You may need to ask each other questions and keep figuring things out. You may have to clarify what you mean until it comes out right. The person you have had communication struggles with may resist the entire conversation (which means you have an entirely different issue). This ain't easy shit. So to give us an even clearer picture of the landscape of communication, let's look at common strategies for sharing what we want to say.

Strategies for Communication

Ok, we got types, and we got styles. What about strategies? Virginia Satir was a therapist and author, often referred to as the mother of family therapy, whose work on resolving communication has been used for decades. She was interested in what people were trying to get out of communication and how that impacts how they do so. That is, she recognized that, while usually preconscious, we are using strategies based on what we are hoping to achieve. She found in her practice as a clinical social worker that change could be effected fairly quickly by identifying issues with communication and working to improve communication effectiveness.

She theorized that our issues with communication are related to the things we needed to do to survive in our families of origin, which we often carry through to adulthood. She identified five communication strategies. The first four communication strategies (placating, computing, blaming, distracting) emerge as shields. The word shield is important, because we've all done some or all of these. I am in no way saying that we are being deliberately shitty when we've used them. I am saying we're being trauma reactive and self-protective . . . even when these strategies no longer serve.

Placaters agree. They tend to do things to please others, to their own detriment. The body posture and voice often demonstrate subservience to the person they are trying to placate. The internet often refers to this as fawning behavior.

Blamers always disagree as a show of power and autonomy. They may demonstrate intimidating behavior in the process, such as a loud voice/aggressive stance/threatening behaviors. Blamers are the most likely to initiate conflict, but that drive generally comes from feeling very alienated.

Computers are freakily calm and rational even in heightened emotional conditions. They strive to be ultra-reasonable which can make them seem unmoving around and dismissive of the feelings of others. A computer is ultra-reasonable, rationalizing and trivializing the content of communication.

Distractors don't follow the subject at hand at all. They may seem nonsensical, but they are really working to get away from uncomfortable topics by trying to get everyone to pay attention to something safer. If a topic shift doesn't work, they may ignore questions, drift off, act sleepy, etc.

Levelers are emotionally balanced. They are assertive about their wants and needs without steamrolling others. This doesn't mean they aren't emotional, but it does mean they're communication is clear regarding their wants and needs and they want problem-solving to be beneficial to all parties involved, instead of aiming for some configuration of "you win" or "I win" or "what problem?" Conflict doesn't feel good, but it takes less of a toll on a leveler's self-worth.

So, clearly the idea is to be a leveler. Satir used this term to describe someone who operates "on the level," meaning with an authenticity and congruence that demonstrates they are trustworthy and engaged. Satir (along with all helping professionals everywhere) demonstrated time and again that we are not our behavior and are entirely capable of recognizing our patterns that no longer serve and adopting new ones.

Leveler communication also quickly derails the four more problematic strategies because a leveler uses clear language, coming to their point quickly and redirecting back to it when necessary. They ask others to speak for themselves, request feedback, acknowledge their experiences . . . all without taking on responsibility for anyone but themselves. Levelers address complicated emotions, are responsive to themselves and the people they are talking to, and do not exert pressure on others to follow their will.

Though, of course, even if we are working to use the most efficacious strategies, we can still get hung up. One of the ideas I use in my practice on the regular is the four levels of communication, to see where within the discourse we get hung up.

Levels of Communication

Last list of this section, I swear! We are all trying to communicate better. Communicating with the "I" statements model is a great strategy for being more mindful of that process. But figuring out where the breakdowns come from the most often is also hugely beneficial. I first heard this model in an online course I was streaming on Neuro-Linguistic Programming. I can't find a reference to it anywhere, so I don't know the origin story (and if you do, please drop me a line). Discussing an idea without the appropriate citation and attribution upsets my little academic heart, but it's too brilliant to not share.

The basic idea is that each exchange of verbal dialog has four levels:

1. What we mean to say. You know, the actual idea you are trying to express.

2. What we actually say. If you are really good at saying only exactly what you mean at all times, I hope you write a book on your technique. For us regular humans, what we have in our minds and what comes out of our mouths is not always a solid match.

3. What the other person hears. Just because you said it doesn't mean they heard it without any filter.

4. What the other person thinks you mean. Even if you said "anything for dinner is fine" and you meant anything for dinner is fine,

your partner may think there is a hidden agenda, or other things going on beyond the words that actually came out of your mouth.

Everyone I have worked with who is struggling with a communication breakdown (with a partner, with family, with coworkers) has a problem in at least one of these areas. Generally, we are high achievers and are activating more than one if not all of them. Figuring out where the breakdown is informs the strategies to repair it.

Let's say you are assigned a group project (fucking hell like no other) and your group is figuring out the task assignments.

1.   What you mean to say. Maybe growing up, you weren't allowed to voice much opinion. Maybe you tend to think your answers are wrong. Maybe you get up in your head about what you want and get paralyzed when trying to communicate. If you don't express yourself well (or aren't great at figuring out what you want), being more measured and considered before speaking or responding

can make a huge difference. Maybe you want to put together the big work presentation but not do the talking part. This is what you intend to get across to the rest of the group, right?

2.   What you actually say. Here is where you gotta use your words. This is easier said than done for a lot of folks. Say you shrug and say, "I'll do the powerpoint or whatever." This doesn't translate well to "Please for the love of everything holy, don't make me do the public speaking part."

3.   What the other person hears. We all have our own interpretations, filters, and distractions. For this example, let's say you communicate pretty clearly: "I get the fear-sweats like whoa if I have to speak in front of other people, I want to stay behind the scenes and put together the powerpoint instead." And someone in the group only hears part of that and writes down that you are going to do the powerpoint, and do the

introduction of the project and be the main speaker. This kind of miscommunication happens sooooo often, unfortunately. It goes back to being lossy—we don't listen well, we get distracted, etc., etc. If this is someone you communicate with on the regular, it's helpful to have them repeat back in their words what you just told them. As in, "I heard you say . . ." In this kind of situation, you may respond with "The fear-sweats are real. I don't want to speak for the group at all, even the intro. Calling EMS when I pass out won't speak well to the project."

4.   What the listener thinks you mean. So many people have had past interactions where all responses were a death trap. They were supposed to mind-read and interpret everything that was told to them, and there was hell to pay if they didn't. A lot of people will overinterpret what you say, so they may benefit from a reminder that you are responsible for your responses and they

don't have to mind-read. If you say, "I don't mind any assignment on the project," and they are worried that they are supposed to figure out your preference, you can remind them that you are responsible for how you communicate and you genuinely meant that you had no preference. If you catch yourself overinterpreting, here's your chance to remember that you are not a mind reader, and people are responsible for what they say to you.

By paying attention to our weak spots in communication exchanges, and actively working to strengthen those areas, we are automatically going to be better at expressing and respecting boundaries. It's an automatic adulting level-up.

SO HOW DOES OUR COMMUNICATION GET FUCKED UP?

*T*here are many things that can get in the way of our understanding of each other. I mean, after all, all communication . . . all of it . . . is cross-cultural. It doesn't matter if we grew up in the same house with the same parents or went to the same schools, churches, camps, etc. We still have different experiences. And a different inner world. And different brains that tell us different things.

It's like the fuego story I mentioned in the introduction, right? That one is easy to notice as a mismatch between what is spoken and what is understood. But what about Tiffany Haddish's story about people telling her she's funny, while using the expression "girl, you stupid"? And how she, someone who struggled with her self-worth about her intelligence, wanted to fight them for calling her dumb?

Tiffany was from the same cultural background as the people giving her the compliment she perceived as an insult. Why is that? Well, she has a pretty significant trauma history which changed her ability to catch context clues.

Because all other issues aside. Cross-cultural issues? Neurospice issues? All of life? These are far more easily mitigated if someone is not navigating the world through the lens of their trauma. And I've also found that the strategies that communication theorists use for cross-cultural issues, neurospice issues, all of it, are the same strategies that work best for trauma-informed communication. Because while we call PTSD a mental illness, it is really a form of acquired neurodiversity. And it is a nervous system injury. So communication works best when it is clear and clean. Let's talk about the research on trauma and communication and some of the research done in this department.

- Unhealed trauma trains you to remain on high-alert almost all the time. When trusting others with our safety seems unfeasible, we go on the defensive in how we interact with others.

- In the process, unhealed trauma trains you to avoid places, people, situations, and topics that activate your trauma response.

- And unhealed trauma trains you to detach and/or dissociate what you can't avoid.

- Unhealed trauma causes emotional dysregulation. Affective issues (mood disturbances like depression and anxiety) is what separates Complex PTSD (diagnosable by the ICD, but not the current DSM) from traditional PTSD. Dysregulated emotions can (and often do) lead to externalizing, such as outbursts of emotional energy, or internalizing, such as struggles to express emotions, guarded communication, or complete avoidance.

- Unhealed trauma can affect memory, especially with recall (forgetfulness). It is also common to lose concentration (in conversation with others or even our own train of thought) and become easily distracted. If the brain is focused on threat detection, it can't perform other tasks effectively.

- Unhealed trauma can cause intrusive thoughts/flashbacks. When we use the word trigger clinically, that's what we mean. This can also interrupt communication, because it means we are no longer experiencing the present moment, but are re-experiencing our trauma instead.

And, if the traumatic experiences were developmental, there are likely to be other effects. That's where the CDC-Kaiser ACE study can help. ACE stands for "adverse childhood events." Meaning, childhood, or developmental, traumas. They are called "developmental" because they change how our brain grows as we continue to age.[2] Research regarding how these types of traumas affect communication would be an encyclopedic series to cover in detail, but the important thing is just to be aware of what trauma-related factors might be coming into play when communication is disrupted.

---

[2] I strongly encourage anyone working in any field that touches upon mental health to get ACE trained. The state of California has an ACEs Aware course that is free online—it's the one I had my interns take when I was still supervising.

Below is a list of some common ways trauma negatively impacts communication skills. But keep in mind, with this depressing list, that the research refers to these issues as delays. Not gone-forevers. Healing work can help us build or rebuild the necessary neural pathways to develop these skills:

- Decreased working memory (how we hold and process information in the short-term, like being told a 6-digit code that we need to enter onto our phone or something)

- Restricted visual processing (how we read nonverbal communication messages or even our ability to recognize other people and familiar objects)

- Reduced attention and concentration (such as struggling to follow conversations or focus on tasks)

- Diminished ability to engage and learn in social relationships (being unable to connect with others and/or be involved in group activities, leading to educational issues and increased social isolation)

- Challenges with processing information (leading to struggles not just with understanding but with solving problems and making decisions based on the information received)

- Lowered capacity for emotional regulation (creating issues in social situations and harming relationships)

- Impaired oral and written language skills (including sentence structure and word meanings)

- Impaired verbal communication (the cultural rhythm of language, articulation, and volume control of our voices)

- Flattened ability to read nonverbal communication cues

So, as we see, trauma doesn't just impact our communication abilities indirectly, it can do so directly . . . impacting every means we have of understanding others and eliciting understanding from others. Past trauma trains our brains to be protective and predictive in order to prevent more trauma. But also to err on the side of caution when doing so, meaning many people end up living in survival mode, unsure how to learn the skills necessary to rewire these responses and live the kinds of lives they hope for.

In the rest of the book, you'll find communication strategies that you can't figure out when all you are trying to do every day is not drown. By learning these strategies now, you are building new neural connections, engaging in post-traumatic growth, and helping your brain manage activation proactively instead of reactively.

UNFUCK YOUR COMMUNICATION

*N*ow that we have all of the nerdy stuff behind us, let's look at the even nerdier stuff. Meaning, working to be the best humans we can be by sharing our world. So before we get into the "try saying it like this instead of that" kinda thing . . . let's start with the "best human we can be" stuff first by focusing on communication basics. Because that defines everything else.

Everything in this part is about the strategies I share with all my clients as the most skillful tools we have in sharing our world. We'll start with the basics and then move into the nuts and bolts of communicating support and consent, as well as communicating through uncomfortable topics, conflict, and even total communication breakdowns.

Communication Basics

The Communication Commandments

Where did these come from? My years of practice as a therapist and coach, as well as what I value and endeavor to bring to my own relationships. When these things are happening, at least most of the time, we are far more successful in both caring and repairing our relationships.

Presume best intent.

This is the starting point rule anytime I am working with couples or families. If you are looking to repair or strengthen a relationship, presume the other party is doing the same. Unless they tell you otherwise, or evidence mounts in that direction. People aren't great communicators, especially when they are struggling. They may say stupid shit that is truly not what they are trying to convey.

That doesn't mean you should pretend everything is fine. It only means exactly what I said: start out with presuming the other person meant to connect not to harm. Ask, "When you said XYZ, I read that as a criticism of ABC. Is that what you meant?" When I ask that question when working with couples and families? Almost always, the person who said something ill-advised immediately becomes horrified and apologetic and then we are able to figure out what they were really trying to share and make the adjustment right then and there.

Now, every once in a while someone will be all, "I said what I said." The intent was harm. Unkindness. Diminishment.

And that sucks.

But when that's the case, you need that information. Not to fight about, but to make a decision about. If someone walks into communication looking to make you feel bad? That's a relationship you need to make some decisions about.

No subtext.

People with trauma histories and people with neurodiversity issues (and especially those of us with both) will tell you that subtext confuses them. You know what I mean. The implicit messages that people do not explicitly state. Like saying "fine" when things are not fine. It's exhausting to try to interpret what people really want when they just won't fucking tell you, isn't it? Even for those of us without these histories, wading through subtext is exhausting.

And what if we stopped? What if—hear me out—if someone tells us "nevermind," we just . . . neverminded? Think back to the four levels of communication thing from earlier. The fourth level is "what we think they mean." But what if we just took it at face value? That puts the onus for clear communication back on the other person. Don't scramble to figure out what someone wants if they hit you with a fine that is anything but fine. If someone says "I'm FINE!" Just say, "Oh good, I was worried you weren't . . . I'm glad you're ok, and let me know if that changes." And the same goes for us. If shit ain't fine, we don't say it is fine while expecting others to figure out what we really want.

When the topic is difficult, take extra care to communicate in a way that the other person says works best for them.
Best way to make communication easier? Ask the other person what works best for them. SO WEIRD, RIGHT? The way I express this in my practice when working with couples is this: "You will have to hear uncomfortable information about yourself sometimes. We all do. If your partner needs to tell you about something that's a problem for them, how do you best hear that kind of information so you can respond skillfully instead of with confusion or defensiveness?"

Some people prefer it in writing so they can think, process, read it a few more times, calm down, and then be ready to respond. Some people get activated by emotional displays because of their own histories. Then the techniques that we talk about throughout this book, like using "I" statements, will work much, much, much better.

Don't say things you don't mean. And do say exactly what you do mean, concrete as pavement.

This should be a no-brainer, but I've found that it isn't. The biggest example I see of this is individuals telling their partners that the relationship is over while frustrated and upset and arguing. And I don't need to tell you how awful it is to hear things such as that on the regular. Because at first, they believe it and get all fucked up. And then they eventually disbelieve it, and it becomes a silly, false threat that doesn't lead to any change or repair. Even if you feel some kinda way about a situation? Speaking to that in a heated moment means you will have a more extreme response. And it's always better to give yourself time to process and make considerations before speaking on a large decision. Huge boulders of decrees spoken in anger are rarely meant.

The two of you against the problem instead of the two of you against each other.

This is especially true of close relationships like partners, dear friends, family members. But it can also be true of other regular relationships, like coworkers and the like. When something is affecting more than one person, solving it together like a team rather than taking shots at each other? Means you actually solve it. If a relationship is being affected by an issue, no matter who is at "fault" for the issue, both people have to work together if the intent is to fix it . . . and ideally preserve the relationship.

Using "I" Statements

Learning to communicate your boundaries more assertively and effectively doesn't require a weekend Tony Robbins retreat. It just means considering effective communication as a skill, learning that skill, and practicing until it becomes second nature.

Try this when communicating to someone else when you are all kinds of hacked off (or all kinds of thrilled, for that matter):

I feel . . . when you . . .

What I want is . . .

You know what this is? Being a grown-ass person who takes responsibility for their own feelings and actions and clearly communicates their needs, rather than blaming other people ("You made me mad!") or doing the freeze-out-no-talking thing ("If you really knew me, you would know this was important right now!").

It's gonna feel all kinds of weird and awkward at first. I've had lots of people tell me that they burst out laughing the first few times they try it. It's just so unnatural, isn't it? Because we don't encourage people to talk like this, taking accountability and responsibility for their feelings.

But we should.

Our feelings are completely our own, and we shouldn't blame others for them. We can, however, ask them for different behaviors that better respect our boundaries. This skill works in regular communication and stays in place even if your convo has leveled up to conflict level. Keeping ownership of your own feelings completely shifts away from the blame game.

You can even take an extra step in acknowledging that the other person didn't intend the distress you felt, for instance, by adding something like the following:

I felt uncomfortable when you made that joke just now. I know you just meant it to be funny and thought I would laugh rather than be upset. But I struggle with jokes about that topic. I would really appreciate it if you didn't tell jokes like that around me.

That's awesome shit right there. And bonus points on this, because other people can't tell you how to feel if you are taking ownership of it. It's not right or wrong, it's just what you feel. Adulting FTW.

Communicating What We Want instead of What We Don't

Cristien Storm's book Empowered Boundaries makes the point that while there is nothing inherently bad about a hard "no" regarding what we don't want, communicating what we do want opens up whole other avenues for dialog and negotiation. A simple example?

Person 1: How about sushi for dinner?

Person 2, Option 1: Ugh, no.

Person 2, Option 2: I'm really in the mood for a hamburger. I'd like to go there if you are interested? Or we could grab takeout from both places and then we can both get exactly what we are feenin' for.

The second option opens up a completely different conversation and negotiation options.

But not all "what we want" communications are sushi and hamburgers. Sometimes a topic requires a level of vulnerability that is really hard to articulate. This means that more than just adhering to a boundary, we have to authentically identify our desires and communicate them more effectively, right?

Example:

Person 1: How about I gag you and tie you up when we have sex tonight?

Person 2, Option 1: Absolutely not.

Person 2, Option 2: What I would really like to explore is prostate stimulation. How do you feel about using a toy designed for that on me?

See how the second option carries far more risk for the asker? I get into more detail regarding these kinds of interactions in my consent zine, using Betty Martin's wheel of consent, but this serves to illustrate how sometimes while a full-stop no is a perfectly acceptable answer, an expression what you DO want can create huge shifts in understanding yourself and communicating that understanding more effectively with the people in your life.

Consider: Who would be a safe person in your life for you to experiment on communicating your boundary about what you do want instead of what you don't want?

Nobody likes to be told no. Being told no sucks. It makes our inner toddler kick and scream, and all those toxic societal messages start to leak out in response. But the word no (or other words and actions that convey it) is one of the most important ways people express boundaries. What if we started paying attention to "no" messages in a conscious way, and dealt with being told no like badass adults? These are some of the strategies that help:

Pay attention to your feelings with self-compassion. If we stuff our feelings, they are just gonna explode out later, like an overstuffed garbage bag. It's ok to think, "Ow, that hurt . . . I was really wanting that to happen."

Put no in its proper place. No is generally the rejection of your offer, not your personhood. Quite rarely is someone saying that everything about you is wrong and unwanted and fundamentally broken. Our inner demons may tell us that when someone doesn't want to hang out with us, but it's bullshit. There are tons of good humans in the world that

I don't want to work with, go to parties with, or see naked. I know you feel the same way . . . and it's important to remember that others can feel that way about you without it being symbolic of something greater.

Recognize the boundary you hit and learn from it. If someone tells you no, they are setting a boundary. This is good information about them and your relationship with them. No is the space where we communicate our understanding of where the boundaries are erected. Communicate this understanding. Don't wheedle or try to convince. Of course you are disappointed, but don't pout around slathered in butthurt. Say, "I'm bummed, but I get it, no hard feelings."

Respecting people's boundaries is how we make our relationships better. People will know they can trust you with their truth and that you will respect them and understand that they aren't attacking your personhood. It makes you the embodiment of safe space. And it also serves to reinforce that if we can do that work for others than we deserve the same work done for us. Win-win.

S.T.F.U.

I have a confession to make. I get super excited about shit and tend to verbally run over people. Especially when I'm being quiet and listen-y at my clinic all day, I get way too jabbery after hours. An ex of mine called me "Mistress Interruptess," which was a nice (and funny) way of pointing out when I was on my bullshit in that regard.

Because I wasn't communicating effectively if I wasn't listening effectively. And I was definitely going to end up unintentionally hulk-smashing people's boundaries if I was being oblivious to what they were saying.

I love Sarah Mirk's book *Sex From Scratch: Making Your Own Relationship Rules.* I was skimming through my well-worn copy recently and found a hot-pink highlighted paragraph that really resonates with the ideas I am endeavoring to share here.

Sarah shares a communicating strategy they learned from a tech entrepreneur named Matthew: S.T.F.U. While shutting the fuck up is something that most of us need to do at some point, his acronym is a little different and is wonderful advice for all kinds of communication. If you are listening differently, you are HEARING differently.

S.T.F.U stands for:

Share Time: Conversation is a two-way street. Being silent and listening is just as important a role as talking. A friend of mine actually saw Matthew's talk on this technique and tells me that he offered a math equation to help people conceptualize how to share time in a simple way. He suggests dividing the amount of time you have for the interaction (say an hour) by the number of the people in the room (say six) and make sure you don't spend more than your portion of the time talking (in this case, ten minutes).

Three Seconds: Give others a chance to continue to speak or jump into the conversation before you begin to speak. That means counting to three when there is a pause in the conversation before making your own verbal contribution.

Find Empathy: Really listen to people . . . not just the content but their backstory. Where are they coming from?

Understanding Is Not Necessary: I really love this one. Active listening is designed to help us better understand others, right? But that doesn't mean we always are successful at doing so. We've all had a what-the-literal-fuck moment in regard to someone else's worldview. It's okay to simply accept it as theirs without "getting" it. And maybe further marination on what they are saying will give you an aha moment later?

Communicating Support

Now moving on from basics. How do we show someone else we love them, value them, and want to show up for them?

In therapy, learning how to communicate support generally starts to come up after people have recognized how their history impacts the ways they show up for others. With that in mind, in this next section, we look at how we can better figure out what kind of support someone needs and even how to maintain connection when things go really south.

What Does Support Look Like for The Other Person?

If a healthy relationship operates as a secure base, we know we have a place to call home when things fall apart. One of the biggest ways you can communicate that you are a secure base is the way you show up when a loved one is going through something difficult. Your role is to find out if they are looking for **space**, **support**, or **solutions**.

You don't have to ask in those exact words. A go-to question may be something like: "Holy shit, that's a lot! Do you need to be left alone for some quiet time to process everything, or would it be more helpful for me to be here with you to listen? And I know you don't need anyone to fix your life, but if you want some help sorting out some options and getting stuff done, I can do that too."

Now this doesn't mean that it's your job to sit there and listen for months on end to someone complaining about the same fucking problem while not doing a fucking thing about it. You can love someone dearly and want to preserve the relationship but be very over their complaints about their shitty boss week in and week out while doing nothing differently. There's nothing wrong with wanting sympathy while processing out loud and organizing your own plan of action. Or even when there is nothing much to be done but having someone else recognize that you are in a difficult place. But it's a far different thing when this is someone's modus operandi about life, and they seem to be gleefully wallowing in their misery and want you to bear witness.

This is where boundaries come in. You can lovingly tell a friend who wants to revisit the same issue where you listen and commiserate for ever and ever and ever that you aren't going to do that anymore. Something like, "I know we've talked about this a few times and I can tell you're really stuck. I think revisiting it is making things feel worse for you instead of better, let's focus on something in your life that doesn't suck or let's go do something together that doesn't suck so you have some kind of suck-free zone in your life."

They may have the type of personality that lends to dramatic responses and attention-seeking behavior. That doesn't make someone a bad person, just one that has learned to get their needs met in a way that is exhausting for those around them. And if you provide attention and support in a new and different way, they'll shift out of that mode far more quickly than you fear.

Or maybe your person isn't a drama llama but they are legitimately stuck. Even so, the amount of venting another person can hear has its limits. When we are having a rough time, we need to express our appreciation and gratitude when people provide that sympathetic support, and then follow up with asking them what's going on in their lives. And we have to remember that our friends are not our therapists.

They don't have the necessary perspective to give us that neutral view, and it may be the kind of issue where finding a therapist or a support group would be more appropriate. It's totally ok to tell your venting friend, "This sounds like a lot . . . are you seeing a fancy professional for support or do you need help finding one who's a good fit for your situation?"

And When It's Really Bad?

So this is about communicating support to a loved one in deep grief and pain, through the huge losses that affect all of us throughout life, when we most need the support of others. I wrote about grief in my book *Unfuck Your Brain* and spent a good deal of time writing about how to support others in deep grief, not just working with our own grief.

Part of what makes it so difficult to effectively support others who are grieving is the fact that we are so close to them. We feel awful with them, not just for them. And we are far more likely to smash boundaries in our attempts to feel better. For example, a friend may say, "Thank you so much for asking but there isn't anything I need right now and I really just want to hide out for the weekend." But we are worried about them and show up with a dozen cookies anyway. This isn't an intentionally unkind gesture and cookies are lovely. But they already said no thank you, and our need to do something got in the way of respecting their boundary. But once we recognize that's our instinct, we can dial it in and use our communication skills so we can be functionally supportive.

The best thing you can do is be helpful only when it's useful to your grieving friends, and not make it about your need to do something. That is, do things that help them feel better, not things that help you feel better. A great way to communicate with grieving loved ones is to say something like this: "If there is anything I can do that makes your life a little more manageable right now, please let me know. I don't need an assignment/something to do because I'm worried about you, but I'm your person for any task that is too much to deal with right now."

And you're thinking, "Ok, but I have a hyper-independent friend who won't tell me when they actually need help and I always find out later." And I'm totally that hyper-independent friend. And my bestie has been wonderful at reminding me that he's there in those situations. If I mention something that didn't get done, he would say, "That's exactly the kind of thing I can help with, if you'd like me to." No recrimination, just a communicative reminder of support.

It's also hard, in these situations, to figure out how much space to give someone who is radio silent. A grieving person is generally not time-aware that they haven't reached out. And you don't want to be obnoxious about it but you also don't want them to feel abandoned. And praise be texting for giving us the perfect mechanism of support. This is where you say, "Hey, I was just thinking about you. I know you're going through it so you don't even have to respond but I just wanted you to know you were on my mind." You can also offer low impact support, like dropping off food but not staying and hanging out and eating with them. Or dropping off a gift card for a restaurant they dig that they can use now or have as a resource later. These are small reminders that communicate it is their turn to be supported and they don't have to perform any role in the relationship in order to receive that support.

Communicating Consent: Boundaries

We can't talk about communication without talking about boundaries and consent. Sorry, ugh, I know. But. Communication is how we do boundaries and consent. I know I've been guilty of nurturing a world of butthurt that would have been easily prevented if I had just used my words. Unless you are a total specimen of perfection, you've probably done the same at some point. Changing how we engage can make all the difference in the world.

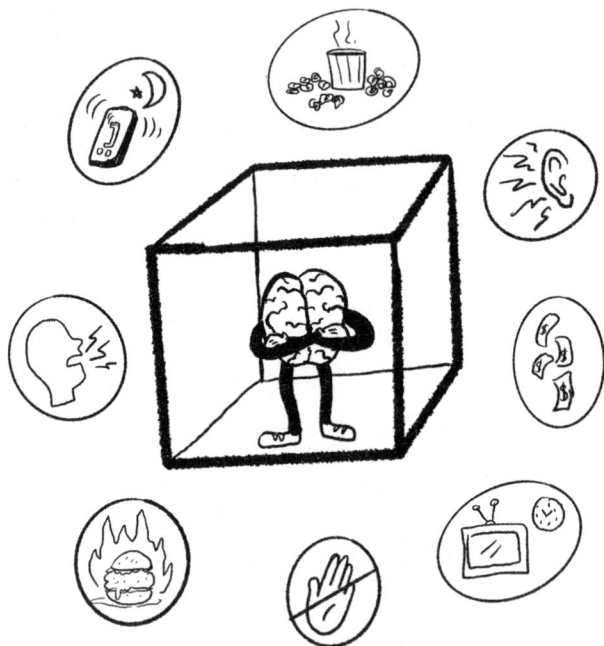

There's a linguistics theory called the Sapir-Whorf hypothesis that talks about how what we think informs how we speak (and we all get that part) and also how the way we speak starts to change how we think. Someone exposed to racist language, who starts taking on some of those linguistic tendencies, will eventually code themselves into overtly racist actions.

The brain is just a huge sponge when it comes down to it. So understanding our language patterns and making active changes in them will create better ways to negotiate the world, and better ways to recognize, uphold, and communicate boundaries.

How Do the People in Your Life Respond to Your Boundaries?

Boundaries are fundamentally relational. And not something we can really avoid since research shows our brains are hardwired for connection. Here's a place to gain some perspective regarding your boundaries-in-relationship. Because we're looking for patterns here, right? To look at how boundaries are working in your life, consider the following questions:

- Which people in your life respect the boundaries that you communicate? What do these people have in common?

- Which people do not? What do these people have in common?

If, generally speaking, most people in most situations don't respect your boundaries, then it's time to look at how you are communicating them. Maybe you aren't expressing them as effectively as you thought. (Good news: you can use the strategies in the pages to come to better communicate those boundaries.)

But if you are struggling more in specific relationships or with specific people who keep blowing past your boundaries, then you might, in fact, be dealing with an asshole, or an asshole-infused situation, like a really shitty office culture. Or systemic power-over injustice at a societal level, because let's not pretend that shit doesn't happen.

Before you apply some smackdown, and especially if you're looking at a newer relationship or situation, consider a few other possibilities for why your boundaries aren't being respected:

1.   This person could have other stuff going on, such as medical or emotional health issues, that make attending to what you communicate difficult for them.

2.   This person might be autistic, making traditional conversation cues difficult for them to suss out.

3.   Maybe the individual is neurodiverse in other ways (e.g., ADHD, traumatic brain injury) and has a hard time attending to relational, nonverbal signals and implicit messages.

4.   The person could have mental health issues that make them so internally focused that they don't have a real awareness of their impact on others.

5.   The person may feel so inferior to you that they don't see how their behavior impacts you.

6.   The person's behavioral compulsions could be so ingrained that they use violating the boundaries of others as a means of feeling more in control of the world.

7.   This person might be an abuse groomer digging in their heels in an attempt to get you under their emotional coercive control.

If the last scenario is the case, you know what you need to do: get out of there. Seriously, get yourself safe. If it's already escalated to violence, please get some support in making a safety plan. I'd start with the National Domestic Violence Hotline, which you can access by calling 1-800-799-7233 or logging into chat with someone at thehotline.org.

If the other scenarios are a possibility, it's time to have a different conversation. Ask the person how they respond and learn best and try adapting your communication style.

Chances are that with scenarios 1–3, you will need to take away any need for guesswork by expressing your expectations as concretely as pavement. Ask for their attention, express yourself clearly and directly, and elicit feedback regarding their understanding. For example:

Hey, friend person, I need to chat with you about something. I recently had a "well, duh" moment when I realized that I have a boundary that I haven't communicated with you. I'm not mad at you, it's totally on me to have told you. I know you're a hugger, and you hug me whenever we hang out together. And I love that about you. But I grew up in a family where I was forced to hug everyone, whether I was comfortable with it or not. Including some people who really creeped me out. Now I feel more comfortable when people ask if they can hug me before doing so. It's a body autonomy thing that's really important to me. I know that will make sense to you and you will respect that, so I feel comfortable telling you the whole story rather than making up some bullshit story about having a cold and not wanting to hug anyone. In the future, please ask me before you hug me and understand and respect that sometimes the answer will be no, but that has to do with me, not you. Does that make sense? Do you have any questions for me?

In scenarios 4–6, you may find that responding to them as a high-conflict person is the best course of action. Check out the section later in this book on BIFF responses; it's a great tool for high-conflict conversations.

Unfortunately, you may be in a situation where you just have to suck it up too. I'm well aware. You have a shitty job you can't afford to leave. Or you have a shitty family that you can't, at this time, extract yourself from. You have to weigh your options before deciding to throw down over a boundary.

This is another place where the flexibility thing comes in. You will find that tolerating others' lack of respect for your boundaries is far easier to manage when you acknowledge to yourself that you are making a choice to maintain the relationship rather than maintain the boundary. It may be the best choice for you at this moment. Remind yourself that this epic dickitude is just slightly better than the alternative, so you are choosing to accept it for right now. This perspective can really help you tolerate how upset and angry you feel. It may also propel you into creating the action plan you need to extract yourself from an increasingly shitty situation, rather than sitting in that slime pool of disrespect and disregard forever.

Questions for determining if a boundary is safely enforceable:

- What kind of relationship do you have with this person (friend, family, coworker, rando at the co-op, etc.)?

- Are y'all on the same level, or does one of you have power over the other (is someone the boss, a person who has societal privilege, a parent that pays the bills, etc.)?

- Is this relationship time-limited (are you stuck with having to deal with this mofo on the regular)?

- What would you like to tell this person if you could communicate everything without any consequence?

- What are the consequences if you communicate those things?

- Are the consequences manageable? Is there a way to make them more manageable?

How to Communicate When We Fail to Respect Other People's Boundaries

We've all had boundaries violated by others and done some boundary violating ourselves. If boundaries are how we communicate our consent, this means that not only have nonconsensual things been done to us, we have also done nonconsensual things to others. No matter how small or innocent an action felt to us at the time.

So while yes, this can range from horrific actions like rape and abuse to the more everyday crappy things we do (like finishing off the last of the ice cream even though you knew your roommate was saving it for later). There are always places where we could have done so much better in terms of demonstrating and communicating a respect for others.

Being an adult means examining the messages we've received our entire lives critically so we can make better and more informed choices for ourselves and the world around us. Recognizing we are the product of our experiences helps us unpack the messages we received in the past, either from family, friends, or greater culture. Part of this process includes dealing with the consequences of having violated others' boundaries. I've had a lot of people tell me that they carry deep guilt for past actions.

Guilt is not a signal that you are an irredeemable shithead: it's a signal that you have work to do. That you now know better and are committing to doing better. And that essential work happens through the process of accountability.

Accountability is the willingness or self-propelled obligation to accept responsibility for and repair the harm caused by our actions. It may mean listening to and holding space without defensiveness for another person's experience of how your actions have caused them harm (which is wayyyyyyy harder than most people think) so you can offer an apology and interact differently in the future.

It may mean doing some big soul-searching, self-examination type work about how you have walked in the world for many years. Individuals who have engaged in substance use find this to be an important part of their recovery. But they aren't the only ones. Those of us who had significant trauma histories will often continue those cycles of abuse and pain, systemically hurting others and ourselves the way they have been hurt. Unpacking generations of toxic, reactive behavior takes a huge amount of work. But that work is how we heal ourselves, those around us, and future generations. You've heard the expression "hurt people hurt people and healed people heal people"? Cheesy with extra cheese, I know. But so, so true. We can't change the past, but we CAN say, "This is where the harm stops."

Accountability work is difficult. But it's essential to having healthy relationships despite the boundary violations that we inevitably do to each other. As brain science bears out, we are a species that is hardwired for relationships. That means we need relationships to survive, but it doesn't mean we always do a good job at them. Accountability, of which communication is a vital part, should feature prominently in our relationships, personal lives, and professional lives.

Reflect on one of the moments I know you've been thinking about where you violated someone else's boundaries. Are you still in contact with them? Do you have the sort of relationship where you could have a discussion about what happened and either request or give an apology? As in, "Remember that time I ate your ice cream? I was thinking about it and I really owe you a sincere apology. You were saving it for when you had a hard day, and then your day sucked even more when it wasn't there. I can't go back in time, but I can do and be better in the future." Notice that this apology didn't include any explanation about why you ate the ice cream or blame for the other person not eating it sooner. It's about healing your relationship, not excusing yourself.

Or if you're asking for accountability from someone else, you might say, "Remember last month when we went out for drinks and I said I didn't want to have more than two beers, but you ordered a few rounds of shots and said, 'Don't worry about it, we're walking home so it's no big deal if you drink them'? I was really uncomfortable with what. I felt pressured to drink more and was frustrated that you weren't respecting my earlier request. I ended up drinking them, then was obviously mad at you about it. We can't go back in time, but I can be better at expressing my boundaries so you can be clearer on respecting them."

Also? This is a personal soapbox of mine, fair warning: you need to apologize without justifying your behavior. For instance, "I'm sorry—I didn't have any money for lunch so I took yours from the fridge," is the opposite of an apology. It's a justification. It's doubling down against their hurt feelings.

Defensiveness about unintended consequences is also unhelpful. "I ran your car into the light pole but I didn't mean to" is frustratingly unhelpful, even if you add a "sorry" somewhere in the mix. Nobody assumes that intentionally running a borrowed car into a light pole was on your agenda. Instead, try, "I'm so sorry I ran your car into the light pole. It's my responsibility to have it fixed." This apology includes language of accountability, which means owning the consequences of our actions, honestly and completely.

This is a real, completely true story of a conversation I had with my late husband. He came in from the backyard and announced that my chimenea (which is a clay fire pot, if you are wondering) was broken. When I asked what happened, he said, "It dropped. And it broke." When I asked where it dropped from he said "Well, I was moving it. And it fell out of my hands. So it broke when it dropped from my hands."

(I know in reading this it seems like a ridiculous explanation, but people explain their actions like this ALL THE TIME once you start paying attention.)

We must have gone round and round for another ten minutes of me saying "So you dropped my chiminea and broke it?" and him arguing "NO! It dropped and broke!"

When he finally said, "Yes! Fine! I dropped it and broke it, but I didn't MEAN to!" I replied with, "Of course you didn't mean to. You're not an asshole going around breaking people's shit on purpose."

Sometimes we intended harm and there is a whole other layer of accountability work to do there, but generally, we're just dumb humans bumbling around and fucking shit up even though we're trying out best. How different it would have gone if he had said, "Babe? I was trying to move your chiminea, and I broke it. I can try to fix it, but since it's clay it probably won't repair well enough to build fires in anymore. I'll replace it when I get paid on Friday."

Just apologizing isn't enough, either. If an apology is called for, do it. If you were the one stealing everyone's lunches at work, ceasing to steal those lunches isn't going to repair that trust. Think about how your actions or words impacted the other person, particularly if your actions were over a period of time. If you argue with your friend every time they tell you what they need from you, focus on listening instead. Make sure you hear and understand the nuts and bolts of their requests and commit them to memory.

Apologizing is a powerful tool for repairing relationships, but it isn't always appropriate. It may not be appropriate or safe to reach out. Or the other person may not be interested in what you have to say. If so, here's a new chance to respect their boundaries. This is something else that we should really consider on the regular when doing accountability work. In twelve-step language, we make amends unless doing so would cause the other person harm. And opening up someone's healed wounds for our own sense of well-being is definitely a form of harm.

A friend of mine really biffed his relationship a year ago and tried to reach out and apologize to his ex . . . who wasn't having it. He told me, "I need to respect her wanting to be left alone. It's the least I can do, right?" Friend-person realized that this was not only a boundary, but his need to apologize was really about making himself feel better and less about repairing the harm he caused the woman in question. By not insisting on further communication, he was actually communicating his understanding of the boundary.

If you think of someone you may have hurt in the past, what do you need to do to make sure it doesn't happen again in the future? It may be as simple as realizing, "I never thought about it that way. Now I know that 'convincing' someone is actually shitty and sketch, and I'm over it." Or it may mean, "I really shouldn't drink that much. I'm far more likely to be a dick to other people when I do." Here's a chance to make a commitment to yourself about your future interactions.

Beyond apologizing when needed and appropriate, it's always more powerful to show change and work for change instead of telling people that you have changed. Visible allyship and peer-to-peer support are critical to the kind of evolutionary change we desperately need to survive. Many recovery programs have people who have worked the program move into sponsorship roles, helping others in the ways they have been helped. Programs like The Forgiveness Project make public the work of accountability and healing. But it doesn't take renting a billboard. It may be volunteering time to a local advocacy group. Or demonstrating your accountability around others, therefore modeling interpersonal effectiveness as a mechanism of social change (ahhhh shit, I just got all political again, didn't I? #sorrynotsorry).

Questions to consider:

1. How, specifically, do you want to improve your respect for the boundaries of others? State this in positive and behaviorally focused terms (For example, "I want to

listen to the viewpoints of others without interrupting in order to understand where they are coming from" is far more doable than "I want to stop being a judgmental asshole.")

2.   What is your reason for wanting to make this improvement? What makes this a personal priority?

3.   How will making these improvements change your life?

4.   How are you hoping that these changes will improve life for people that you care about?

5.   What are your best practices for moving forward? What are the actionable steps?

Ok, so now that we have a better idea of your own boundaries: that was a fuck-ton of emotional work, wasn't it? Ugh, yeah. Let's go ahead and finish off the navel-gazing by looking at how you respond to the boundaries of others.

1. Generally speaking, do people tend to respond positively to you?

2. Do they tell you they feel comfortable sharing with you? That you hear them without judgment?

3. Do you have people (or at least one person) in your life with whom you are able to have deep and authentic exchanges of ideas and feelings?

4. Are you able to maintain these relationships over a long period of time? What kinds of situations make it hard for you to respect the boundaries of others? Is it with certain people? Or when people are making certain decisions that cause you concern?

The first three questions are a good self-examination of whether or not you are able to maintain relationships. If you struggle with the boundaries of others, it will start to eat away at all of your interpersonal relationships. Let's be honest.

Do you know anyone who is bad at boundaries but somehow still maintains healthy relationships? I don't.

If you read the first three questions and had an "oh fuck" moment, that doesn't mean you should put down the book and immediately start emotionally self-flagellating, ok? We generally learn good or bad boundary-setting from those around us. If no one modeled healthy boundaries for you in the past, how were you supposed to learn? And since no one is handed the boundaries manual at birth, a lot of us have to figure it out later. As you start being mindful of boundaries in your interactions, I bet you will see serious, positive changes in your relationships overall.

The fourth question is more universal. Because I promise we all have situations where we struggle to respect other people's boundaries. It might be with family members you care about, when you see a friend making the same dumb decision for the ninety-seventh time, or when someone engages in a behavior that you've previously seen lead to a bad end for yourself or others. Those kinds of situations can really make it hard to respect their boundaries.

And it's ok to communicate that. To say something in the vein of:

"I'm having a hard time respecting your boundaries right now because I'm really worried about you. I don't want to start bossing you into doing what I want you to do. It might be better if we don't discuss this particular issue because I can't really be impartial."

It's the nicest way I can think of it to avoid a "Your new bae is a piece of shit! Break up with them!" conversation that's only going to get you into trouble.

It's also ok to ask for clarification on what level of support someone is looking for. For example, I struggle with the boundaries of my adult kiddos. Makes total sense, right? I still want to parent them. When they ask for my advice, I ask straight out: Do you want the mom answer or the supportive-adult-in-your-life answer? This gives them the opportunity to let me know how flexible their boundaries are about my interference in the situation and has probably saved us from any number of fights over the years.

When No Remains No: When Do You Need to Justify Your Boundaries?

Let's talk about the complicated terrain of when and how we communicate justifications for our boundaries to others. (I think this means we are now getting into a PhD boundaries class, don't you?) I've found in my private practice that the one thing that feels worse than setting boundaries is the need to legitimize them once we set them. If your boundaries have been really permeable in the past, it's easy to fall into the trap of overexplaining as you firm them up, even in situations that are not high-conflict.

In her book *Empowered Boundaries*, Cristien Storm explains how we sometimes get hooked into feeling a need to defend or justify our boundaries.

You know, the relational labor we put into the overexplain of our boundary.

When I read that, my first thought was of Pema Chodron's definition of *shenpa*. The Tibetan word is usually translated as "attachment," but I prefer Chodron's translation, which means "hooked." It's that feeling of going down a well-worn path or getting caught in a record scratch that creates a continuous skip. Chodron describes it as that feeling of being trapped in a situation that doesn't feel good, causing us to tighten up and shut down.

Boundary work can trigger shenpa just like any other situation. The hook, in this case, is feeling the need to justify a boundary we are setting. Or convince someone else to understand our boundary. Advocating for ourselves can feel really uncomfortable, and a lot of people get an urge to justify their self-advocacy.

Boundary shenpa is the result. Being in our feels about setting or holding a new boundary is so uncomfortable, we go into our headspace instead. And start intellectualizing the whole process to ourselves and the person with whom we are setting the boundary. This prevents us from being authentic with ourselves and with others.

Justifying a boundary isn't always a bad thing. It depends on the situation, right? If a friend asks if I can attend her event, I can say no as a complete response. Or I can say, "I'm sorry, I'm actually in the office that day . . . I'll be exhausted afterward and will really need to go home and rest." Some justifications are relationally relevant, which is not the same thing as boundary shenpa.

Boundary shenpa occurs when "no, I'm not comfortable with you borrowing my car" turns into an overexplanation, or even falsehoods, to justify your no. "I'd totally let you use my car, but I have errands to run/the brakes are spongy/etc, etc." Because we don't feel comfortable with our own boundary and don't want to upset the other person or have them think we're being shitty, so we get into justification mode.

What's the antidote to boundary shenpa? The Tibetan word here is *shenlock*. It refers to a renunciation of an old pattern. When you notice that physical response of tightening into a need to over justify, try to recognize the habit in yourself with loving-kindness, and respond with the new boundary-setting habit we are working to become more natural. Practice how you are going to communicate your boundaries and how you are going to respond if someone DOES get butthurt. Some ideas:

• "No, I'm not comfortable with you borrowing my car."

• "I see that you are upset by my answer, and I respect that you are upset, but I'm not going to lend you my car."

• "Be that as it may, my answer is no."

Recognizing these patterns and changing our interactions isn't one of those things where we have a huge breakthrough and make a seismic change, then never have a problem again. It took years and years to develop our ways of communicating, and it will take a while to learn to do it all differently.

And this process is like the train of dominoes, where they are laid in a row and knocked down in a particular order. Old communication patterns that no longer serve us are some of the first dominoes we target.

Communicating Through Uncomfortable Topics

We've all had moments when communicating about certain topics feels out of our depth. In this section, we'll cover ways to communicate through the most sensitive of subjects: sex, religion, politics, addiction/mental health recovery, food, and money. Obviously this isn't an exhaustive list of hot topics, but they are consistent biggies for most of us.

Communicating about Sex

Conversations around sex are nerve-racking for most humans. After all, this isn't something society encourages us to do. But the only way out of Mordor is through Mordor, and the quickest route toward positive sex communication is through conscious effort to solve problems together: remember the "us vs. the problem instead of us vs. each other" rule.

For instance, saying no thank you to something you don't want to do isn't mean. It's clear. And clear is always the kindest option.

The biggest obstacle to overcome in saying no, and often even to a conditional yes, besides our own internal people pleasing instincts, is to make sure we are differentiating that the no is a rejection of an offer, not a rejection of the other person or our relationship with them. Having a few back-pocket scripts can be hugely beneficial if you struggle to express yourself. Such as:

1. I'm super into you, but that particular activity is not on my menu. It's like shellfish: most people love it and others are allergic.

2. I'm ready to get started. Do you prefer to put on a condom yourself or is it sexier if I help?

3. I can tell you had a long day at work. Let's take a shower together and get refreshed before we get into bed.

4. I love how into receiving from me you are—it turns me on. But receiving from you is also a huge turn-on, and I'd like more of that in our life. Without making it a weird scoring system or something, how can we be more equitable in sexytimes?

The Feedback Burrito

Sometimes we realize something isn't great for us, during or after the fact. This is utterly normal and natural and you aren't expected to know everything and express it perfectly. And you are allowed to realize that something you were game to try is not something you want to continue to do. Or that you still like the idea but y'all didn't do great on the execution. One skill I learned in my doc program,[3] was how to give feedback to new interns in a way that incorporated all the things they were doing really, really right with the area that we needed to work on. It's slightly more complicated than sandwich feedback (positive, negative, positive), because

---

3 From Dr. Heather Trepal. I'm saying that for the sole purpose of embarrassing her by mentioning her in a book with the word *fuck* in the title.

the human brain centers negative information so strongly (for survival reasons).

This means taking a little extra care in communicating, knowing that brains can be total negativity trolls, by encouraging while also requesting change. Hence the term burrito because the formula is: positive comment, positive comment, place we need to do a little work, positive comment.

Example:

I loved it when you did . . .

And . . . was smokin' hot.

One thing I think would work better if we did it differently is . . .

I think it would be even better if we . . . instead of . . . next time.

And all in all, I really enjoyed . . .

So, when all is said and done, we are putting the request for something different rolled up with lots of praise. Now there's some good sex communication FTW.

Communicating about Religion

My mama's side of the family is hella Irish Catholic. Like so Catholic, if you married into the family you had to convert. And everyone did. Until my aunt said, "Nah." She was Jewish. I mean, she still is Jewish. Everyone was super worried what that would mean . . . and then their worst fears came true. The year we all gathered in Washington for Christmas at another's uncle's house? And everyone was going to midnight mass? My aunt declined, truly respectfully. And my uncle chose to stay back with her; mass wasn't that important to him and his wife was. Which even as a teenager, I saw immediately as the right and respectful decision.[4]

The others clearly did not. Now, there was no shouting and yelling about it, but there was a lot of snark from the midnight mass attendees about how they knew this would happen. (Insert grumbling, petty comments here.)

Fortunately, there was no more drama than that. Even if all of that was unnecessary, many

---

4 Straight banger, Uncle Kelly. Good on you.

people have it way way worse with their family and loved ones—especially when one person's religion declares that the choices of others are wrong/sinful/evil.

As we look into what it means to communicate well about religion, the first thing I want to remind you of is this: You don't have to eat shit for people. You don't have to afford them more respect than they are affording you. You DON'T. But as a through line of this book? Sometimes we don't have nearly as much choice as it seems from the outside. For any number of reasons. Or you may really love these people despite these differences and want to find a middle ground.

As Sarah Schulman writes in her book *Conflict Is Not Abuse*, you don't owe anyone this level of relational labor. But the only way to shift us back to belonging, respect, and mutual understanding? Being considerate, recognizing where people are coming from, finding common ground, and setting aside (at least in certain circumstances) points of disagreement. This section is about doing those things and becoming more skillful in your disagreements around religion with loved ones.

How to Shut Down Shitty Comments

How to deal with shitty comments about religion: this question is one I hear all the time in my work. Again, at least my family kept their midnight mass snark amongst themselves rather than spewing it at my aunt and uncle. But how the hell DO you respond when Uncle Timmy tells you that God thinks you're an abomination? Without causing a food fight that ends with all the delicious cream cheese mashed potatoes smashed onto the wall instead of in your belly? Well, with as much calm as possible. Which means preparing your responses ahead of time. Here are some of the scripts I have found most helpful in this type of communication situation.

- "That makes God seem like kinda an asshole. And I think there is too much beauty and love and grace in the world for that to be the case."

- "I think the most important part of religion is the call to love and care for others. Those are the messages I try to focus on in my daily life."

- "I guess we won't really know until we get to the Pearly Gates and find out who Peter lets in, eh?"

- "This is definitely one of those 'agree to disagree' moments. Let's move on."

- "Oh, you know me . . . just out there making everyone worry about my heathen ass! Thanks for keeping me on your prayer list!"

Communicating about Politics

The root of the word political is polites, which just means "citizen." Politics refers to the affairs of the citizen in society. (Do with that knowledge whatever amuses you.) Obviously, politics has far-reaching effects in our world and lives, so how do we talk about it?

In 2023, the Benson Strategy Group (BSG), did a survey about how we handle politics at family gatherings. Only six percent of Americans report arguing with their family over politics (and this was mostly Gen Z and Millennial respondents). Fifty-nine percent of people avoid talking about politics at all. BSG asked how people were feeling about the political climate in general with a recent change in the makeup of congress and the then-looming presidential election. The answer was no surprise: seventy percent of respondents were feeling ungreat about the whole enterprise. BSG used the term "gloomy," to describe our feelings that politics has become even more contentious and divisive.

Fair points all around.

But what is interesting is that respectful, open conversations can make a huge difference in bringing us back from extremes. Earlier, in the religion communication section, I mentioned Sarah Schulman's book *Conflict Is Not Abuse*, which is an excellent resource applicable to political conversations as well. Another great and relevant resource is the work of political science professor

Dr. Taylor N. Carlson, who has written several books on political stances, partisan politics, and communication around these issues—who has found that we are generally better people for healthy discussions about differences.

Also, as I said in the section on religion? You are not required to do relational labor around politics to shitty people who are denying your existence. I say this a trillion and three times because I fucking mean it. There will still be at least one email from someone who said, "I cAn'T bELieve yOU ToLD me TO bE pOLIte to My assHOle uNCLE!" I will refer you back to this page reminding you I said no such thing. Protect your peace. But if these are people you love? And you want to connect with? And find common ground with? This is where change occurs.

Dr. Carlson shares research that shows time and again that when we reduce belief in stereotypes, we reduce polarization and hostility. Political identities are having an increasing venn diagram overlap with our social identities. In other words, we are voting more and more by affiliation versus party platform and record—all of us, anywhere on the progressive to conservative spectrum. And that isn't always the best decision for any of us on that aforementioned spectrum. And positive changes and openness to ideas and perspectives? Those happen in the context of relationship. We really do want to get along with our people, so what does it look like to communicate about politics in ways that invite others into a different dialog?

How to Engage Respectfully Around Politics
The baseline for respectful political communication? Express your stance not as an unimpeachable truth (even if it is, I know, but still) and ask the other person about theirs.

Then, agree when they're right. For example, maybe they say, "Your candidate did [insert ungreat thing]." Your response? "Yes, I agree. I didn't like that either. I believe in holding all elected officials accountable. That behavior is something that needs to be addressed and rectified."

Also, when necessary, disagree politely. As in, "I saw that same news story and was upset too. But it turns out that situation was misreported, and actually . . ."

Another important piece of this communication puzzle? Don't call people liars. First of all, when someone says something untrue in the context of politics, they usually think they are telling the truth based on their belief system and the information fed to them. Remember that the most extreme shit someone believes isn't so much about the beliefs themselves. It's about the person's general deep unhappiness with the world as it is—and the fact that they are looking for simple solutions to that unhappiness.

Calling someone a liar is also an invitation to a fight, right? Instead, you can say "I've seen several studies that come to a different conclusion." Or even, my favorite, "That is not a true statement." The latter one works well because you aren't nodding and agreeing with bullshit, but you aren't making an accusation about someone's character . . . saying a statement isn't true is different from calling a person a liar.

What if the Political Beliefs Are . . . Cultlike?
Now, when it gets to the political beliefs that are the most extreme, there may be no conversation to be had about those beliefs. At least until the person holding those beliefs is starting to see some cracks in the foundation.

An important note here: this section isn't positioned against any particular group. It is no secret that I am a raging progressive, and I will freely admit there are people on "my team" that believe and say profoundly stupid shit. Wherever you fall on the political spectrum, it's hard and imperfect work to be open to new information that changes your thoughts and positions.

But what do you do when a loved one is clinging onto cult-like political beliefs? Many of the mental health professionals that specialize in cults find that talking about topics outside of a cult-adjacent person's belief system is the place to start. Things like the weather and football and other safe topics.

The idea is that cult-like beliefs grow in an echo chamber and in isolation. For example, Covid lockdowns created the perfect conditions to grow extremism. So, if we can remain in connection, we are creating space for radicalized loved ones to reach out when they start to question their belief system. Simply put, by staying present in their life in some small way, you give them the opportunity to see other ways of living in the world. Through you, a loved one.

The TV show *New Amsterdam*, covered this topic gracefully using Q-Anon as an example when the chief of psychiatry, Iggy, explained to a son that the best way to help his Q-Anon–affiliated father is to not challenge or agree with the beliefs of his father, but to be there when he's ready to challenge them himself. Cults tell you anyone who argues is an outsider not to be trusted, right? So telling your loved one they are wrong is only telling them you aren't to be trusted.

Humor can be a great way to transition away from cult-like political talking points. For example, saying, "Not here to talk about that. I came to fight about the Toronto Maple Leafs chances at a Stanley Cup this season. And bruh, what's up with that trade?"

Presence and understanding, not arguing, are the first steps in deprogramming. The research shows that when people leave cult or cult-like groups or thinking patterns, it was their own disillusionment saying "Waitaminnit." Not the words of friends, families, or therapists. So keep the lines of communication open with safe topics, and you may yet see your loved ones return to reason.

Communicating about Addiction Recovery and Mental Health Treatment

I am well aware of how difficult it is when the people who installed your buttons start pushing all of them. And if you've looked for strategies for dealing with them in the past, you likely ran into a lot of, "Go for a walk! Embrace spirituality to be a better person than they are!" Or whatever. When in reality, it's far more helpful to be as concrete as pavement in what supports you.

You're allowed to get better. And allowed to get better in the ways that make sense to you. Right now, of my clients in recovery, there are multiple paths. A couple are doing a traditional twelve-step model, a couple more prefer Wellbriety, and an equal number are doing moderation management. The variations of supports individuals are using for their mental health treatments are even more diverse. Meds, herbs, ketamine, mushrooms, neurofeedback, other tech, etc. Hell, even the type of therapy that I do with them is different based on their needs and preferences. Not everyone wants to do yoga with me, right?

Which is all to say you don't have to defend your journey. You don't have to explain yourself to anyone not paying your bills. I'm proud of you, even if your family isn't. It's entirely ok with me for you to say, politely:

"I'm working hard on being my healthiest self and it's a personal journey. Thank you for showing your love through your concern, but I'm doing ok and want to focus on us hanging out right now, not that part of my life."

Or, less politely:

"Your questions and comments are both nosey and unkind. None of this is your business and I am asking you to cease these comments and questions or I will leave."

You are also more than allowed to do the things you need to do to stay in recovery when surrounded by people who are picking away at your wellness. Find a local meeting, if meetings are part of your recovery. There are plenty of online ones as well. Have a sane(r) person that you can check in with.

A sponsor, a recovery coach, a therapist, a friend. Anyone who knows your journey and is there to support you.

Do the things that help you manage stress—what helps you better manage cravings and impulses to use. If it's working out, do it! I Eat in a way that helps keep your blood sugar stable. If you are on medications, make sure you have the dosages you need with you and use any supports you need to remember them.

My neurospicy peeps especially know that as meds wear off, the temptation to use goes way up. You may be used to rawdogging reality and keeping shit together through sheer willpower. But certain situations devour willpower within minutes. Give yourself some support.

Communicating about Food

Food plays such a big role in our lives, so it makes sense that the number of people who are living with/working to heal from an eating disorder (or disordered eating) is a large number. Research says about thirty million people, and that's likely an artificially low number, and only accounts for people who had met official diagnostic criteria and are actively seeking help.

Most everyone in industrialized society has had a toxic relationship with food at some point in their lives. The average American will be on an average of 126 diets in their lifetime. Which is one of those numbers that is so nuts to me and so telling about how toxic our culture is.

And the stressors that influence our eating patterns, at least in the short-term? Two big ones are experiencing conflict and feeling lonely. And many people find these issues compounded by "well-meaning" comments about their appearance, what they are eating or not eating, or any other sensitive subjects (especially those that are identity-driven). And our dietary patterns do affect our mental health.

Please consider how you best handle stressful situations, and try to create some pockets of that self-care for this situation. If you need support, ask for support. Especially if you are in eating disorder recovery. Have a peer who knows that journey be available to call or text if you are in danger of restricting, binging, or punching the shit out of any family members that want to comment on your body. A study done by researchers at Columbia University found that this level of support helped the most with lessening anxiety and depression.

There's a reason people in substance use recovery have sponsors. People who get it are priceless.

Also enlist allies that are present and that will have your back at fraught gatherings. Having a cousin jump in and say to Uncle Chuck, "oh, we're not talking about people's bodies this year, Chuck, let it go," gives you allyship and keeps you from having to do all that relational labor and defense for yourself.

Chuckles may still be a total toolbox, but having someone in your corner lessens the impact of it on your mental health. Cousin has your back, then you can say, "Hey, Uncle Chuck, I heard you caught some amazing walleye last month on your fishing trip . . . what's your secret?" Chuckles will be thrilled to pontificate about fishing and will move on from the size of your ass in those jeans. Or whatever bullshit he was up to.

Communicating about Money

No matter what your relationship dynamics are, if you have a partner, a close family member, or anyone else you share space with, statistically speaking, money is causing some kind of conflict. If you are married? Money is the number one thing that couples argue about and the number two cause of divorce. So let's talk about talking about money with the people we love.

When It Is a Partner

The two most important things for communicating about finances with a partner? (1) Having upfront conversations about how you will allocate money together and (2) a commitment to financial fidelity. The latter is just like sexual fidelity—it means whatever rules you agree on for the relationship, you both honor them. A budget made with a partner is a contract. Nobody is perfect, but continuous fuckups are a pretty big hit on a relationship.

I work with a lot of couples going through separation and divorce, and sketch shit about money comes up over and over again as a relationship-ender. Small things like constantly going out to lunch with work buddies when there was a commitment to bring sacked lunches in order to pay down debts, or trips to Target where the packages stay hidden in the trunk of the car. Or big ones, like money being hidden and accounts being emptied.

If you're having money conflict in your relationship, the first step is to figure out what kind of help you need. Are your relationship's financial problems communication shit or chronic financial infidelity shit? Even if you're not sure, I'd high-key recommend starting with therapy (couples counseling if you can convince your partner to go). All the practical financial advice on the planet won't help if one member of the agreement continues to say one thing and do another.

Also, therapy pro-tip: Financial conflict is definitely a type of relational conflict, so if you have health insurance that covers therapy, it'll be covered. If you are looking for free or low-cost options in your community, lead with the fact that this is a relational conflict, rather than saying you are looking for financial counseling.

But even if you aren't hiding things from each other, how do you negotiate money in your partnership when, say, one of you is an overspender and one is an underspender? Or if you have different values around tipping, or different priorities in paying down debt or what to save for, or whether to save at all?

First, you gotta create a budget y'all can live with. Like separately, without breathing down each others' necks to figure out your priorities while your partner does the same. Then sit down and share your results.

Start with where you agree and plan around that. Even if the only thing you agree on is that paying your rent is better than being evicted.

Then negotiate on the stuff where you disagree. You know, the fun stuff like buying a new house versus using the extra for trips. I know, this can be rough. One tip: It can be helpful to discuss your short- and long-term goals as individuals and as a team. (When money is the relational point of contention for couples and families in therapy, these goals are the conversations that I start with.)

After that heavy lifting has been done, one of the big things that really helps is making sure that everyone in the relationship has a guilt-free discretionary fund, where what you spend it on isn't challenged. Even if it's ten dollars that you want to be able to use on onion rings or puffy stickers, having some financial fun is important. It could be money that's put aside into a separate account or cashed out for walking-around, but it needs to be all yours. Feeling like you're under your partner's microscope is no fun for anyone. It's a partnership, not a parent-child relationship, after all. (I mean, unless that's your kink, which is totally cool by me.)

It's also helpful to set a dollar amount on other household expenses, where purchases over that amount are discussed. This may be for small things, like the grocery budget, and larger things, like buying a new bike or car. Giving your partner the chance to weigh in on, "I found this thing for $200 more than we planned on spending, but I think it makes sense because . . . what do you think?" will save infinite fights later, trust Auntie Faith.

If your communication is good and y'all are in a good same-team mindset, you'll be able to do more of what you want with money: together.

Other People Fucking Up My Finances

Partners aside, how your friends and family spend their money—and expect you to spend yours—can definitely impact you and cause you stress. Buddies go out drankin' all the time? Family that buys expensive-ass gifts and you are expected to reciprocate? We have all had an experience of getting pulled along with some spending that we hadn't budgeted for, really couldn't afford, and will resent later.

It's most helpful to realize in advance which of these situations are the ones that you are most likely to get stuck in so you can organize your counterattack in advance. If you have a plan in place and a script to rely on, you are far less likely to end up pulling out your wallet and fucking up your whole financial month.

Some ideas to get you started:

"I'm doing an austerity month challenge, so I have to pass on the concert this month. But I've been all up into my free-event research, and the museum is free next Sunday. Wanna plan a paintings-and-picnic date with me?"

"We've been looking at our long-term financial goals and made some changes so we can achieve them at a faster rate, so we've decided to opt out of the family gift exchange this year. Honestly, our favorite part is just hanging out with everyone. Please don't feel the need to buy us any gifts . . . Auntie Enid's chess pie is what we live for, and we promise to bring the lemon bars!"

"That sounds like a blast, but I'm determined not to bust out my plastic this month . . . can I skip the dinner and join y'all for the movie part after? That'll save me a ton of fundage and honestly, I want to finish off these leftovers before they spoil so I can be proud of my frugal adulting prowess."

"I get mad at myself every year that I can't go on vacation, and I'm determined to make it happen this year . . . so I'm gonna pass on the outlet mall trip. I know me, and I don't make good choices once I have the opportunity to buy my hundredth grey sweater."

These are all matter-of-fact examples that focus on your financial goals with zero shame attached to other people's choices. And that's the way it should be, right? If people wanna drop some bills on tequila shots, that's one hundred percent their right. But being thoughtful and practical about your choices may end up starting a trend with some of your people. Your friends may say, "Oh! What's an austerity month? Maybe we could all do that together and support each other!" Maybe your family will say "Good idea! Let's do a cookie swap or a white elephant exchange rather than spend fifty bucks on brandy snifters!" Or whatever. Brandy snifters are a thing, right? I dunno. The point is, you aren't asking anyone to do anything different because of your spending changes.

In my office, I say several times a week that it isn't that people aren't willing to change. We are just unwilling to be changed. Frame your financial practices as your thing, rather than something everyone should do with you. Because even if that is one hundred percent not your intent, people will read it as such unless you state quite clearly that you don't give AF how they spend their money. If you make all these changes and they're still sitting around with their brandy snifters, whatever. You aren't pushing your choices onto others and are working to find ways to stay connected without dropping a ton of dough. Be like the vegan who brings an amazing plant-based chili to a potluck and offers no side-eye to all the meat-based dishes other people bring.

But Faith, you're thinking. What if they are shitty about it? Or passive aggressive? Yeah. People do that shit. And it's about them, not you. And if it's their shit, you don't have to take it on. It's totally cool to recognize and validate that they don't like what you're doing and then do it anyway. "Be that as it may, I'm sticking to my plan for now. If it doesn't work out, you can laugh at me later!" is a cheerful, argument-ending answer.

The other big issue we tend to get into with our friends and family members is when they want to borrow money. This is tough. You've done a lot of work on getting your own shit together and then you have people around you saying, "Cool, hook me up." I was raised in a culture where caring for your community is a core value. So I believe in that. And I get it. But caring for your parents or siblings shouldn't come before caring for yourself and/or planning for your own kiddos.

I'm a big believer in not lending money I can't afford to lose. I would rather give someone the money they need outright and not set up a resentment trap for the both of us. I know that for some people, paying back a loan is really important to them (that's me, I'm some people), so I won't insist on making it a gift, but I still operate as if the money is gone and spent and not going to be returned.

I also don't want to get hitched into an ongoing problem. A family member recently asked my husband to cosign for a line of credit so they could deal with a credit card collections demand. After my husband and I discussed it, we offered the money to get them caught up on the current credit card instead of having our name on a janky payday-type loan.

If you love someone but don't really trust them to spend money on what they say it's for, then is it possible to just buy them the thing they say it's for? If a family member can't make rent . . . can you write the check to their landlord rather than fork over the cash? It's your money; you get to make the rules and set the boundaries.

When someone tries to hit you up for money, from a communication standpoint, it's ok to take a minute to respond. Tell them, "Let me look and see what's possible" or "Let me talk to Boo about what bills we have coming up and get back to you." That gives you some breathing space so you don't feel pressured into making an immediate decision. Then decide what you can and are (or aren't) willing to do and make that offer.

Communicating Through Conflict

Conflict exists in relationships. This is healthy and normal and means you aren't a pushover. But in the thick of it, we often feel like it's the end of the world. Conflict can bring us closer together. But in the moment, it doesn't feel like it, especially since most of us have had zero experience with the healthy expression of differing perspectives in our lives. But like everything else I talk about in this book, healthy communication through conflict is a learnable skill.

To nod back to relational-cultural theory for a minute, I consider all of these topics to be falling under what Jean Baker Miller called "waging good conflict." Dr. Miller was a huge advocate for staying connected through conflict by remaining compassionate and respectful while keeping our own values, ethics, integrity, and boundaries at the forefront.

"Waging good conflict" refers to the process by which we move away from the more traditional Western models of conflict management (you know, someone wins and someone loses)—many of which we learned within our own families growing up. Waging good conflict involves being open to listening to understand, not to respond. Which operates as a model that we hope the other person responds to, encouraging them to treat us with the same level of respect. Relational-Cultural[5] theorist Dr. Linda Hartling frames this level of connection through the lens of human dignity. She states that waging good conflict isn't something that comes naturally from within us, but is co-created in relationships founded on respect and an authentic desire to understand those around us.

Please don't misunderstand me to be saying that this means you should tolerate truly awful and harmful behavior out of compassion. I think the reverse is true. If we are compassionate to others while remaining self-aware, holding our center becomes easier. We're far less likely to be manipulated because we are less emotionally bound up by someone else. We can maintain a respectful connection far longer. And we can detach, as needed, with love.

---

5 Relational-Cultural Theory is a therapeutic framework that includes both the understanding that external social norms cause or contribute to many mental health issues and that healthy, supportive, validating relationships play a significant role in our healings. RCT is my practice framework.

Who Do I Want to Be in the World?

As stated above, a big part of communicating effectively—especially through conflict—is operating from your own moral center. Meaning, you act from a place that is congruent with the kind of person you want to be in the world. Even though everything we do and every interaction we have should operate from this place, we rarely think about what that really looks like (which is probably why we so often end up tilting at the wrong windmills). The things I hope you will consider as you move through this section, and throughout conflicts in your life, include:

- What do you want to stand for? What do you believe in?

- What personal attributes and positive characteristics do you want to demonstrate to yourself and others in the world?

- How will you know when you are successfully living your values?

- How will you know if you aren't?

• How will you know if your priorities have changed and you need to recalibrate?

Resolving Conflict

Now that we've looked at the individual moral center we operate from as humans, we're going to start looking at what it means practically to communicate through conflict. Because even the world's best communicators still have conflict. If the goal was never to have conflict, that would be easy. You would just have to be a total doormat and give people whatever they want all the time. But if you don't want to be a doormat, the goal isn't conflict avoidance, but conflict management.

When things go sideways in your relationships, consider the following questions and strategies:

Is It Intentional?

Is the other person intentionally fucking with you? Like deliberately disrespecting your time, resources, needs, and desires? Like, "I know we had dinner plans but I went out drinking instead because fuck you"?

If it's the latter, you have every right to be mad. But also? What the actual, literal hell are you doing engaging with this person? If they have no fucks to give about what's important to you, get out. Believe what they are showing you about who they are. Call your bestie to request sofa-surfing privileges, pack up your pooch, polish your tiara, and move on.

Fighting is worthless here. Because you are being treated like you are worthless here. Don't fight with someone who has made it clear that they don't care.

Who You Really Mad At, Cupcake?

Remember learning about Freud's defense mechanisms in Psych 101? He may have snorted too much coke, but he was right on about that shit. Displacement is a defense mechanism where we attack the safe target rather than the real cause of distress. Of course you can't tell your boss that his mother was a hamster and his father smelt of elderberries. So you get home already riled up and ready to rumble. Boo tells you they forgot to pick up your dry cleaning and you find yourself spewing venom like a champ.

If you know you are ripe for a fight, like after a hard day, do what you need to do to decompress in a way that doesn't involve sniping at others. And warn those around you that you are wound tight. It's totally ok to say a discussion needs to be put in the parking lot for the rest of the day—just tell your partner that's on you. Something to the effect of, "I'm so upset I'm afraid I'll be hurtful or mean in ways that I don't really feel. And I know I won't communicate well right now. I'm gonna go soak in the tub and figure out why I'm so upset, because I don't think this is all about you. Can we talk about this later?" The big thing is actually setting a date for later—don't use this as a sidestep technique to never have difficult conversations.

Humor Rather Than Snipe

My husband is often frustrated that I suck at hanging towels up to dry. I tend to leave them sitting in the sink. I'm trying to be better at that, but I had years of living alone and not sharing that bathroom with anyone. And it doesn't bother me. I'm probably gonna use that towel to mop up the floor before I throw it in the laundry, anyway.

(Which also grosses him out, but that's another story.)

If I forget to hang up the towel, he will tease me into remembering rather than yell. "Who hates to hang up towels?" And I'll wave my hand in the air and say "Me! Meeee!" It's obnoxiously cute, but it is way preferable to a stupid fight over a stupid thing, right? I remember to go hang up the towel and neither one of us feels irritated in the process.

Now, someone else having this same conversation might mean it in a mean, snarky, or demeaning way. By contrast, my husband is being silly about it, and I take it in kind. The important point is that you find a way to communicate without the sniping, and finding avenues that rely on your shared sense of humor can really help. I've been working with a couple on communicating better with "I" statements. I made a joke about how "I feel you're an asshole" is not an "I" statement. That cracked them up so much that, "Well, I feel that you're being an asshole" has become their in-joke that defuses tense conversations.

Beware the Horsemen

Relationship researcher John Gottman is famous for saying he can predict divorce with ninety percent accuracy. All his research led him to develop what he terms "The Four Horsemen of the Apocalypse." Of his four horsemen, he has found one to be more destructive than all the others. Along with criticism, defensiveness, and stonewalling, the biggest relationship destroyer is the horseman of contempt. Contemptuous language—communication that demonstrates you don't respect your partner—not only becomes a pattern of negative dialog between the two of you, it reinforces you in thinking about and seeing the negative in your partner.

Gottman also says that the ninety percent accuracy rate is predicated on people not changing. If you notice that what you are feeling is not just frustration with your partner's choices, but an actual disgust with them as a human being, ask yourself if this is something that you can change with a shift in perspective. If not, you have a pretty good idea about the path you are on.

Ask for What You Need and Negotiate on Preferences

Communicate your needs (the areas around which you have rigid boundaries) and ask your partner about theirs. If you can't honor these needs in each other and don't think that you would ever be able to, time to abort mission. If someone's need for safety outweighs your capacity to give, that is neither your fault nor theirs. Maybe they have a trauma history that needs more work before they can regain equilibrium. It just is what it is. And like everything else about the human experience, our needs may change over time. Admit when yours change and ask for a renegotiation. Be vulnerable enough to ask for support.

And then there are wants. We all have our preferences and idiosyncrasies. Most of them aren't worth fighting about. Being our own weird, individual selves doesn't mean we are intentionally fucking with our mate, it just means we have years of behavior patterns that are really hard to change. (Ever try to give up tacos for Lent? You feel me, right?)

Mr. Dr. Faith and I are pains-in-the-asses in a million different ways, but battle stations are only activated when there is a cost involved beyond irritation. I have a toilet paper roll holder that hangs over the side of the toilet tank. Mr. Dr. Faith hates the thing because he has to twist around to reach the roll. He prefers to have the roll sitting on the counter next to the toilet (what kind of monster does that???). I don't like that because it gets damp there. Guess what? We have two rolls of toilet paper in the bathroom. One sitting on the counter and one hanging on the holder. Boom.

What things tend to be your relational sticking points? For a lot of people, it's how money is spent. That may mean having an agreement on "allowances"—coming up with an amount that each can spend without checking in with the other based on what you can afford and your financial goals as a couple. Sex troubles? Try out some of the sensate focus exercises in *Unfuck Your Intimacy*. Parenting teenagers? Ugh, good luck with that one. But also, *Unfuck Your Parenting* (coauthored with the amazing Bonnie Scott) will at least give you some commiseration for your predicament.

No matter how big or small, look at the actual cost of the issue before you decide how to proceed. It's amazing how much can be let go when you do that.

Is it Netflix and chill night and you want pizza but boo wants Chinese? Just get both.

Honestly? My goal in life is to have my house be a peaceful abode. I want it to be my favorite place in the world. My spouse feels the same, so we work hard at setting up our relationship so we maintain that peace. It's a good goal for all of us and helps us communicate better through conflict.

Conflict Communication Tool: Collaborative Communication

Another great tool in conflict communication? Nonviolent communication (NVC), a very process-focused system, designed to shift conversations to collaboration. The goal of this form of communication is setting a tone of "power-with" another person instead of "power-over."

Toward this goal, NVC focuses on language itself. Because it is very easy for us fallible humans to perceive the words of others as threats. Threats spur us into power-over reactions, meaning we are looking to win a fight, not to connect and honor needs and boundaries.

Dr. Dian Killian, an NVC consultant and coach, defines four steps of collaborative communication as a way to express with authenticity and receive with empathy. Or, to use a more Dr. Faith–type verbiage? Generally speaking, people aren't out trying to act shitty. We are human, fallible, fuckups. And friendships are seen as the relationships that are easiest to extricate ourselves from, so we are far more likely to tap out than wage good conflict. Here's a super nutshell version of NVC:

Observe/review: Listen to understand, not to respond. Then demonstrate that understanding with neutrality (meaning, without judgment). "I heard you say . . . Did I get that right? Miss anything?" This helps prevent the conversation from getting heated, or at least from getting heated so fast. It's about reflection and clarification. (Instead of "you're a fucking idiot because . . . ")

Speak to your emotions: There is a subtle difference between "I feel confused" or "I feel sad" instead of "I feel hurt" or "I feel disappointed," which can help open the dialog further. Many people say "I feel . . . " then share an attitude, belief, or thought. Such as, "I feel you aren't listening to me." NVC techniques also focus on the expression of emotional turmoil rather than emotional blame, as much as possible. This can be tricky when your emotional response is in direct relation to someone's behavior toward you. And this doesn't mean lie about what you're feeling, but feelings are complex and bringing them to a more global position may help.

Recognize the unmet need: NVC founder Dr. Marshall Rosenberg felt that emotional turmoil existed in response to an unmet need. He identified nine universal categories of needs: sustenance, safety, love, understanding/empathy, creativity, recreation, sense of belonging, autonomy, and meaning. So in this step, we are matching the expressed feeling to the unmet need. For example, a friend seeming angry at you may actually be struggling for a need for autonomy, which may or may not even be related to y'alls relationship.

Make a request: This is where, after all parties are feeling heard and understood, a request that connects to the unmet need can be offered for consideration. Requests work best when they are positive and concrete. Even better when they are about something that can be addressed immediately, not in the nebulous future. Requests in this paradigm are about what we want and not what we don't want. "Stop doing XYZ" brings out stubborn resistance in most everyone. And the word request is also important. Demands awaken our inner toddler that screams no at everything. The question I always get is, "What if they say no? What if they say they can't commit to showing up on time when we have concert tickets?" And the answer is, they are telling you something about their relationship with you and you have a decision to make. If they don't honor your request, you have to decide if you can live with that or if that's a dealbreaker for you.

NVC is a more complicated process than some of the other communication strategies I share in this book. And it's ok if it feels like a lot. Even just using the first step of the process can be incredibly helpful in working through conflict. And I can tell you, as a person whose job is to communicate, and help others communicate, the rest of it becomes easier with time and practice and is an incredibly valuable skill.

Conflict Communication Tool: Objective Effectiveness

When dealing with conflict and other tricky communication situations, consider using objective effectiveness, a term used in dialectical behavioral therapy to break down how we can best get what we want in a relationship. The acronym DEAR MAN is a great mnemonic for remembering the best ways to be objectively effective without being a manipulative shithead.

Describe: Clearly and concretely say what you want. Even people who know us super well don't read minds, you know?

Express: Share your emotions while taking responsibility for them. "I feel . . . when you . . . " is far more effective than "You made me mad."

Assert: Being assertive isn't dickitude, it's honesty. "I don't know if I'm feeling up to it" is a hint, but "I'm exhausted and want to skip the party this evening" is assertive.

Reinforce: When people do the thing you ask them to do, thank them!

Mindful: Don't get sidetracked by off-topic disagreements. Stick to what issue you are trying to resolve.

Appearance: Demonstrate confidence in how you present yourself. Even if your words are assertive, people are less likely to take you seriously if your body language isn't.

Negotiate: Be open to compromise—relationships are give and take.

Tools for When Negotiation Shuts Down

Most of the communication tools in this chapter work in power-with situations where everyone in the conversation has each others' best interests at heart. But there are tons of situations in life where there's a conflict, be it about where to get coffee or how to regulate nukes, and there isn't existing trust in the relationship or maybe you're dealing with a high-conflict person, someone who is freaking out, or someone who truly doesn't care if there's a mutually beneficial resolution.

BIFF Responses

A powerful tool for these situations is the BIFF Response—Brief, Informative, Friendly, and Firm—paired with avoiding the 3 As—Advice, Admonishment, and Apologies. These are tools from Bill Eddy's High Conflict Institute and I teach them to people on the regular. They are great tools for handling conflict and also with situations that are emotionally charged in general.

If you are in the process of communicating better boundaries with someone for the first time, it's going to feel emotionally charged since it's all weird and awkward and new for everyone involved. Having a bit of a recipe will help a ton. Try this one. (Add extra garlic if you're feeling sassy.)

Brief: Don't give any extra info. Don't overexplain. The more you write or say, the more fodder you are giving the aggrieved party for their battle, yeah? Let's say you got an angry missive from your boss, accusing you of jacking the keys to the dumpster. Instead of writing an eight-paragraph defense, try a brief, factual response: "I clocked out two hours before closing last Thursday, so I didn't carry out the garbage that day and I never used the keys."

Informative: Don't focus on their incorrect statements, focus on your accurate ones. No sarcasm, no negging, no remarks about the other person's personality, ethical choices, etc. We are looking to end the conflict, not throw down about who the real dumbass in this scenario is. In the same work example, you might add the information, "In order to refresh my memory, I double checked the calendar. I wasn't the person who closed that day, it was Xander."

Friendly: I know, it doesn't seem fair that you have to be nice when someone else is showing their ass. The best way of coming out of the conflict unscathed is to not match hostility with hostility. This doesn't mean fake nicey-nice . . . just civil. You are far more likely to get a neutral response, if not a positive one. Going back to the work example, you could phrase it as something like, "Hi, Sarah! Xander and I did both work last Thursday, but I clocked out early because it was so slow and Xander closed by themself, so I don't know where the keys to the dumpster ended up."

Firm: Be firm without being threatening. Don't make comments that can invite more discussion (e.g., "Let me know if you have any questions" or "I hope you agree that . . . "). Back to Xander the key-stealer? You could close with, "I wish I could be of more help, hopefully Xander will be." Think like Forrest Gump. As in, "That's all I have to say about that." If you need to get a decision from someone and can't end the discussion here, another feature of "firm" is offering two choices so you don't have continued over-discussion.

If you get more communication after you have already BIFFed your response, you can either ignore it or broken-record your BIFF response with the same keywords and even less content until they give up.

Another Bill Eddy trick for BIFF communication is to avoid the three As: Advice, Admonishments, and Apologies. So let's look at those as well:

Advice: You don't want to give anyone advice on how to manage themselves or the situation they are ramped up about. They are already hot under the collar, so you won't get anywhere. I know I don't hear much when I'm butthurt—that's a pretty universal response. Notice that rather than telling Sarah to check the timecards in my example, I said, "I double checked the calendar and confirmed . . ." That avoided giving her advice on how to do her job. She will realize she should have done so herself once she calms down, so it's all good.

Admonishments: You may want to offer corrective feedback, but just like advice-giving, this isn't the time. The point of a BIFF response is to defuse an emotional conversation and end it for the time being. So avoid anything that makes it sound like you are explaining their behavior to them like they are a naughty child. Again, with Sarah the manager, imagine the continued battle if you had said, "If you had acted like an actual manager, you would have checked the schedule before having a rage fit at me"?

Apologies: Authentic apologies are a good thing. But when everyone is activated, it is not the time for them. Apologizing can give the other person something to blame us for, extending the conversation. "I'm so sorry I don't know what happened to the keys" can let Sarah continue to blame you for her ridiculous insistence that you are somehow responsible. A more gentle "social apology" can be helpful to diffuse the issue, if you want to add that to the mix, however. "I'm so sorry you are having to deal with such a frustrating situation with everything else on your plate!" is a show of commiseration and empathy that doesn't connect you to the blame game and doesn't give Sarah any more ammo.

I know, I know what you are thinking. No matter how boss you are at BIFFing your communication there are some motherfuckers who aren't gonna hear shit from you. Even if you added interpretive dance to the mix, they are so wrapped up in their bullshit they are determined to hear everything you say through that worldview. And in those times when absolutely nothing you do or say will lead to effective communication.

Sometimes you can't stand your ground, even politely using BIFF statements for a multitude of reasons. Maybe they are family members on whom you are financially dependent. Maybe it's a shitty boss at a shitty job that you can't afford to quit. No matter what your circumstances, I am well aware that if "just walk away" were really that simple, everyone would do it.

The following two skills focus less on communication and more on how to protect yourself from someone else's onslaught . . . which is sometimes the only way we can set a boundary.

The Pane of Glass Trick

Are you stuck with motherfuckers who push every last button? One of the tricks I've found that has really helped me is to imagine a clear pane of glass between me and them. I can hear and see them, but their emotional bullshit stops at the glass.

This is especially helpful for us Counselor Troi empath-type people. We can respond to the content of their words and actions without being emotionally drained by whatever forces are driving them.

And for those of us whose empathy leads us into doing more for others than we should (like rescuing, excusing, or caretaking that isn't healthy in the long run for anyone involved), the pane of glass trick can help us remain proactive instead of reactive in a difficult relationship dynamic.

The Grey Rock Method

Another trick for dealing with boundary-busting individuals—or just toxic, shitty situations in which someone is being harmful—is the grey rock method.

A blogger who goes by Skylar on the now-defunct website, 180Rule.com, developed what she calls the "Grey Rock Method" as a tool for convincing abusive individuals to leave you, by making yourself as boring and nonresponsive as possible. You essentially become a grey rock. The more boring you are, the less fuel they have. You are essentially training them to consider you an unsatisfying conquest.

This is a tool that I had unconsciously put into practice as a teen and can testify to how well it works.

I had a grandparent who commented frequently on my weight and body shape. I remember him picking up my arm when I was about 14 and declaring, "You ain't got no wrists!"

My response? "Mmmmm, ok."

The conversation ended right there, due to my complete lack of reaction.

One of my interns does on-call work for a local hospital that tends to be perpetually short-staffed and operating in chaos. Her supervisor was blowing up her phone, wanting to pick up shifts outside her availability. I coached her through a BIFF response, but her supervisor continued to rant . . . trying to guilt my intern with comments like, "I don't have any to cover! I don't know what to do! I really need help!"

My intern responded with, "Yeah, that's a lot" and then stopped responding. Eventually the rant ceased . . . and the haranguement was never made mention of again. If my intern had continued defending herself, her responses would have been used as proof that being short-staffed was her fault, not the supervisor's.

Communicating in Systems

You know what this means. Business settings, school settings, government agencies, on the phone with the electric company trying to keep your power turned on until you get paid on Friday. The stuff where speaking fancy can help you get what you want.

There's a concept from business communication research that can be helpful here: the differences between horizontal and vertical communication.

Possible dirty connotations on first glance aside, horizontal communication just means talking with your colleagues. Our language in these situations tends to remain informal. For example, if you are assigned the same shift as a work buddy, you can totally say something like, "Bestie, respectfully, not happening, I'm swamped AF over here" when they ask for help with their shift tasks.

By contrast, vertical communication, in the business world, is top-down communication. And this is where we are far more likely to communicate formally. When a supervisor tells you to help them with their shift tasks? The response is prolly gonna be different as in: "This is what I have on my task list for today. If I help you with yours, we will need to reprioritize my workload to make room. How would you like to reorganize our deliverables?"

This section focuses on vertical communication, expanding the definition to any situation where someone has more power than you. Or at least a level of power that you are wanting to access for your benefit. So not just your boss or professor. But also the clerk at your local government office or the nice lady at the electric company you are trying to convince to give you three more days to pay your bill. Or the frazzled barista that has been fending off Karen bullshit all day that you want to convince to remake your drink.[6]

---

6 The customer is always right—in matters of taste. We don't usually include those last four words. If someone wants their house painted with zebra stripes. It's their house and their taste, not the painter's business. If they want it painted for free? That's the painter's business.

These interactions also fall under the domain of vertical communication. Which we have all been culturally trained to formalize. While that is changing (very slowly), being able to speak with more formality greatly enhances your chances of getting shit done when navigating top-down systems. Knowing the rules helps you better decide when to break them, after all.

Context aside, all business/organizational communication has one or more of the following three goals: instrumental, relational, or identity.

Instrumental goals use communication to complete an objective. (Communication in service of getting shit done, so to speak.)

Relational goals help strengthen or weaken our relationships in the workplace.

Identity goals shape how someone is perceived.

Now, communication researchers say more than one goal could be in place at a time. And I would say, for peak effectiveness of getting shit done, all three goals should be in place all the time. If we are trying to accomplish a goal. Say, using the example of getting three days grace on your light bill, giving you time to get you paid and make a payment before it is turned off? When you call in to make your case, your goal of getting the grace period is better served if the customer service rep likes you and perceives you as a good and deserving person.

Let's face it, humans are judgmental motherfuckers. We are always sorting our fellow humans in the categories. We can work hard at overcoming these judgments, or at least trying our damndest to base them on facts instead of stereotypes and vibes. But our tendency to judge is a reality of our survival-based primitive brains.

So let's use the three-day extension example.

Customer Service Rep: Good morning, this is Rowan. How can I help you today?

Me: Good morning! I really need a three-day extension on my power disconnect notice. I get paid on Friday and can pay it then!

Customer Service Rep: I'm sorry, we have sent you multiple notices over the past two months. That was the final notice.

Now this is a perfectly polite request, right? It wasn't shitty or Karen-y. The focus was instrumental. And the request was declined, equally politely and accurately to the situation. Still, I can't not have power for the week and I have to find ways to get up and go to work anyway. And now I have to pay to have everything turned back on, as well as late fees and the bill itself. And I don't have enough money to do all of that. So what happens if we add relational and identity strategies to this situation?

Customer Service Rep: Good morning, this is Rowan. How can I help you today?

Me: Rowan, good morning! This is Faith Harper, and I am really hoping you can help me figure something out. I apologize if I sound stressed and anxious. You have nothing to do with it, but I am super stressed and anxious about my shut-off notice, and I am sure you can hear it in my voice.

Rowan: Thanks for that, I've been there too. What's up?

Me: I lost my job a couple months ago. I just started a new one, which is great but I don't get paid until Friday. I am hella behind on my light bill and that's on me, but I am finally starting to get caught up, I'm working all the overtime I can get! Are there any options or programs to extend my shut-off notice for three more days so I can pay it as soon as my direct deposit hits on Friday?

Rowan: Been there too! We don't have a ton of options in that regard, but I can tell you there is a law that prevents us from turning off your power if you have a medical issue that requires you to have power. Like if you use a medical device that has to be plugged in?

Me: I have asthma, does that count?

Rowan: That is definitely a condition that can be exacerbated by the heat! It isn't always approved, your doctor will have to fill stuff out. But I can mark you down as applying for that program and send you the forms. They won't turn off your power for a bit, expecting you to send in the forms for REAP assistance. That will buy you time, and honestly, not a bad thing to actually apply for in case you ever need help in the future.

Me: Rowan, you are a lifesaver!

Rowan: Happy to help! Is there anything else I can assist you with?

Me: Can you patch me through to your supervisor? They always hear complaints, and I'd love to make sure you get your flowers for saving my ass. I'd like to at least leave them a nice message about your quality customer service? What's your last name?

This may seem excessive, and likely extra effort for something that won't work. But as an official old person who uses these strategies, I can safely tell you these strategies almost always do work. This conversation creates a relationship, in which you recognize the humanity and the role of the person answering the phone, knowing this is someone who tends to see some of the worst of human behavior.

YOU also take responsibility for both the fact that you are behind on your bill and you are upset that you may lose services, instead of being defensive and argumentative . . . while showing the steps you are taking to get caught up.

(And yes, I entirely agree that every human being should have what they need to live . . . that was the point of creating society. Everyone is deserving of food, shelter, and all other material supports. But that isn't an argument that works well in call centers. You really do have to demonstrate that you are especially deserving of Rowan's support. Then you show them they were right to do so, by making sure their boss knows they provided great customer service.)

But like all communication, working with systems is complex. Since there isn't a formal recipe, here are some ideas I want you to take from this:

Treat all people like people. Pay attention to someone's name and use it when appropriate.[7] You

---

7 Don't do the weird saying their name over and over car-dealer-salesman shit. Be authentic and human in your use of someone's name.

made the convo person to person . . . not person to entity-representative. Also, if you have a visual (in-person, on video chat, or whatever), you can find other things to notice and comment on. I swear I got assistance swinging some extra financial aid in my doc program, just by complimenting the necklace of the lady in the bursar's office. It doesn't have to be slavish fluffing, either.

It's just noticing.

If we are using the "remake my drink" example, you may say something to the barista like, "I can see you're slammed and working your ass off. I'm so sorry to add more to your workload, but can you remake this for me? I hate being that person, but it didn't come out the way it usually does." That's noticing. We are recognizing and connecting to the humanity of others. Not treating them like NPCs in our personal universe.

Also? If you are really trying to get something done, you should be keeping notes. Like I do when I have to contact federal financial aid (necklace lady hooked me up, but I still gotta pay it back). I write down the name of the person I am talking to, the date, and the important points of the interaction for my own records. Again, names matter!

And having their name lets you go back and give them their flowers when they do help you. And I don't mean dangle it over their heads like, "Help me and I'll give you a baller Yelp review." Do it because it is the right thing to do. Do it because hardly anyone ever does that. When I took an extra eight minutes to praise a postal worker to her supervisor last year, it was because she helped me get my passport in time. I won't need another passport for ten years, so it isn't like I'm gonna need to lean on her again. But the financial aid lady? Whose supervisor got an email from me hyping her up? I got the financial aid I needed, no questions asked, for the rest of my time in grad school. So, yes, bonus points. Either way, you will have an ally if you need one again later.

(Too bad I can't talk my way out of paying it all back, or I'd give that a go too.)

The more attention you pay in these scenarios, the better you will get at reading the person you are interacting with. Sometimes a quiet introvert responds to less energy, and you being soft-spoken and giving them space keeps them from being overwhelmed. But sometimes you'll find one in the wild that responds well to a bit of extrovert adoption energy—making them a friend by cracking a few jokes (not at their expense!) and building up the relational goal part of the process. If you are building the relational goal up to that point, then the conversation is more horizontal and you can be more informal.

Again, it's more a vibe than a recipe, but keeping in mind the three goals and attempting to tag in all of them can make a big difference in getting stuff done.

Self-Communication: Reframing Toxic Self-Talk

I couldn't let you get through the entire book without at least one small section on self-communication, now could I? Most of our communication is from our own dumb brains. And those of us who didn't grow up in the greatest of circumstances often have internalized those voices as our own.

So when my clients are talking ugly to themselves about themselves, I ask, "Whose voice is that?"

And they will always say, "Mine!" And I respond. "Sure, it is now. But the brain doesn't start out being so nasty to itself. Before it became your internal dialog, whose external dialog was that? Who talked to you like that?" And it was a childhood parent or caretaker every time—the people entrusted to nourish and care for and grow our small little bodies and brains into loving and competent adults.

So many kids didn't have their bodies abused growing up, but did have their hearts and minds abused with this kind of correction. And as we grow up, that voice becomes our internal voice.

Now, these voices are our thoughts. And they are referred to as automatic thoughts or automatic negative thoughts (ANTS) for a reason. They are wired in so young that they happen instantaneously. And that's ok. We aren't responsible for our first thoughts. They are as immediate as touching a hot stove and yanking our hands away.

You are, however, responsible for your second thoughts and your first behavior. Capturing the ANTS and reframing them using cognitive-behavioral therapy will help you pivot to a more skillful behavior (instead of a vagal-activated fight/ flight/freeze response).

Here is how it works. When you catch yourself saying something toxic (and yes, you can totally do this on paper or in the notes app on your phone), note it and then consider either a more accurate or at least a more balanced, helpful message. An **alternate** message challenges the original toxic message entirely. A **balanced** message acknowledges a fundamental truth, while focusing on managing it in a more empowering way.

Toxic Self-Talk: OMG, I am such a dumbass, I can't do **anything** right!

Alternate Response: I wish I had done better. But, hey, I'm really good at learning from my mistakes and trying again. Let me think about a different approach to this problem. And for the record, there are plenty of things I get right!

Toxic Self-Talk: I really like that person, and they have no interest in me at all. I must really suck.

Balanced Response: I've tried making a connection, and I'm not their cup of tea. Or they have other stuff going on and don't have space for me in their life right now. I'm going to focus my time and attention on the people who are interested in spending time with me so I can remember that there are plenty of people who think I'm a fantastic cup of tea!

Both alternate responses and balanced responses are designed to be more gentle and self-compassionate in the face of a nasty inner dialog. If the message is just plain wrong, tell yourself that. If it is fairly accurate but simplified and self-recriminatory, then you shift it to something that is more complex and complete to the situation.

Because we aren't looking to self-gaslight, just to be as fair and considerate to ourselves as we would someone else.

Compassionate Letter to Oneself

You can also engage in a practice of compassionate self-communication through journaling. This is a short-interval exercise. In other words, you aren't meant to spend more than five to fifteen minutes on it, and it is one you can repeat over days and weeks if you find it helpful.

Ernest Hemingway entreated us all to write hard and clear about what hurts. I think many people would take that to be unflinching, and I think we all expect unflinching writing to be critical. I think an unflinching view, however, is a kind one. It is balanced. It recognizes both intent and complications. It encourages accountability instead of defensiveness.

Think of something you are unkind to yourself about on a regular basis. Something you beat yourself up about. Reflect on how this particular issue makes you feel. Guilty? Embarrassed? Sad?

Now focus on what you would say to someone you love and admire who is going through the same thing and feeling bad about themselves. Maybe they (you!) really did mess up something, but you know they aren't a bad person, just a flawed and struggling one. How would you support them? How would you show them compassion for their struggle while helping support any changes they are looking to make?

Now, tuck the letter away for a couple of weeks. Write more letters or different topics in the meantime if you want, but let each letter simmer a bit after you complete it. What happens when you go back to it later? What is different in how you interact with this issue and yourself?

CONCLUSION

$\mathcal{W}$riting about communication seemed an insurmountable task. But, in reframing my own negative self-talk (see what I did there?) I reminded myself that I didn't have to write the encyclopedia of communication throughout human history. All I had to do was share some hard-learned skills around how communication gets disrupted and strategies for getting it back on track while rewiring (healing!) the communication processes in the brain that got pretty battered in our early years.

Even when communicating solely for the benefit of someone else, we are participating in our own healing. Recognizing we can be kind and skillful and proactive even when distressed? That shit helps us recognize our own self-worth as well as the inherent worth of every being around us. Good communication helps heal trauma. And we deserve any strategies we can get our hands on when doing this work.

Healthier relationships? Firm, kind boundaries in the face of fuckery? Treating people like people with their own struggles and complexities? Those are all markers of a healed soul. And we all deserve one.

REFERENCES

Arnone D, Patel A, Tan GM (2006). "The Nosological Significance of Folie à Deux: A Review of the "Literature," *Annals of General Psychiatry*. 5: 11. doi:10.1186/1744-859X-5-11

Bick, J., & Nelson, C. A. (2015). "Early Adverse Experiences and the Developing Brain," *Neuropsychopharmacology*, 41(1), 177–196. doi.org/10.1038/npp.2015.252

Centers for Disease Control and Prevention. (2021, April 6), "About the CDC-Kaiser Ace Study." Violence Prevention Injury Center. cdc.gov/violenceprevention/aces/about.html

Center for Health Care Strategies (2019, January 23), "What Is Trauma-Informed Care?" [Video]. YouTube. youtu.be/fWken5DsJcw

City of San Diego (n.d.), "Trauma Informed Resources," Commission on Gang Prevention and Intervention, sandiego.gov/gangcommission/directory/trauma

Family Violence Prevention Fund (2004, August), "Identifying and responding to domestic violence: Consensus recommendations for child and adolescent health. Futures Without Violence. futureswithoutviolence.org/userfiles/file/HealthCare/pediatric.pdf

"Five Types of Communication," Graduate College of Drexel University (n.d.), drexel.edu/graduatecollege/professional-development/blog/2018/July/Five-types-of-communication/.

Haskell, L., & Randall, M. (2019, January 1), "Impact of Trauma on Adult Sexual Assault Victims: What the Criminal Justice

System Needs to Know," SSRN. papers.ssrn.com/sol3/papers. cfm?abstract_id=3417763

King, J. (2009). "Emotional Abuse: The lack of Emotional Safety as an Internal Indicator in Abusive Relationships," Prevent Abusive Relationships, preventabusiverelationships.com/ articles/emotional_safety.php.

National Center on Domestic Violence, Trauma & Mental Health. (2011, August), "Tips for Creating a Welcoming Environment," Creating Trauma-Informed Services: Tipsheet Series. nationalcenterdvtraumamh.org/wp-content/ uploads/2012/01/Tipsheet_Welcoming-Environment_ NCDVTMH_Aug2011.pdf

National Center on Domestic Violence, Trauma & Mental Health (2019), "Creating Trauma-Informed Services Tipsheet Series," nationalcenterdvtraumamh.org/publications-products/ creating-trauma-informed-%20services-tipsheet-series-for-advocates/

National Child Trauma Stress Network (NCTSN) (2008, October), "Child Trauma Toolkit for Educators," nctsn.org/resources/ child-trauma-toolkit-educators

National Child Trauma Stress Network (NCTSN) (2020), "Child WelfareTrauma Training Toolkit: Supplemental Handouts Questions for Mental Health Providers," nctsn.org/print/1145.

National Child Traumatic Stress Network (NCTSN) (2017, July 17), "Safe Spaces, Safe Places: Creating Welcoming and Inclusive Environments for Traumatized LGBTQ Youth," [Video]. YouTube. youtube.com/watch?v=8zNbQ_8KRew

OASH (2021), "Meaningful Youth Engagement," Office of Population Affairs. opa.hhs.gov/adolescent-health/positive-youth-development/meaningful-youth-engagement

Robert Wood Johnson Foundation (2013, May 12), "The Truth about ACEs," [Infographic] rwjf.org/en/library/infographics/ the-truth-about-aces.html?cid=xsh_rwjf_pt

Rowe, K. (2020), "Improving Provider Confidence and Partnership with LGBT Patients through Inclusivity and Education.," Doctor of Nursing Practice Projects, 5. scholarworks.seattleu.edu/dnp-projects/5

Sashko Gramatnikovski, Aleksandra Stoilkovska, and Gordana Serafimovic, 2015. "Business Communication in Function of Improving the Organizational Culture of the Company," *UTMS Journal of Economics* 6 (2): 267–279.

Schladale, J. (2013). "A Trauma-Informed Approach for Adolescent Sexual Health," Resources for Resolving Violence, foster-ed.org/wp-content/uploads/2017/01/A-Trauma-Informed-Approach-for-Adolescent-Sexual-Health-2013.pdf

"Speech, Language, and Communication Needs in Youth Mental Health," orygen.org.au/Training/Resources/Neurodevelopmental-disorders/Clinical-practice-points/Speech,-language-and-communication-needs-in-youth/Speech-language-communications-needs-in-YMH.aspx?cxt=.

Substance Abuse and Mental Health Administration (SAMHSA) (2019, August 2), "Trauma and Violence," U.S. Department of Health & Human Services. samhsa.gov/trauma-violence

SAMHSA's Trauma and Justice Strategic Initiative. (2014, July), "SAMHSA's Concept of Trauma and Guidance for a Trauma-Informed Approach," ncsacw.samhsa.gov/userfiles/files/SAMHSA_Trauma.pdf

Violanti, M. T. (2017). "Business Communication," *The International Encyclopedia of Organizational Communication*, 1–14. doi.org/10.1002/9781118955567.wbieoc016

Washington Coalition of Sexual Assault Programs (2012), "Creating Trauma-Informed Services: A Guide for Sexual Assault Programs and Their System Partners," WCSAP, nsvrc.org/sites/default/files/publications/2018-04/Trauma-Informed-Advocacy.pdf

APPENDIX: TOXIC RELATIONAL STRATEGIES IN COMMUNICATION

*W*hat are cognitive distortions? A thought we had that we decided to hold on to as a truth . . . even when it's not that true, and not that helpful. It's a story we've become attached to and act from. And it ends up causing problems. Typically when we read about cognitive distortions and common thinking errors, we are focused on the types of thought patterns that lead to a spiraling of depression and anxiety. But there are other kinds of thinking errors (and their accompanying behavioral patterns) that have just as large an impact on ourselves and an even larger impact on our relationships with others. The phrase "toxic relational strategies" means not just how we think in certain circumstances, but how we interact with others based on those thinking patterns.

These are behaviors everyone is capable of. Everyone has engaged in some of these strategies at some point in their lives. And we have all been victims of these strategies. Not just from perpetrators of abuse, but from otherwise good people who engaged with us in unhealthy ways because they thought that was the best way to meet their needs. The difference is in the degree in which we undertake them.

The purpose of this exercise is to look at patterns of interactions in our own lives, examining the toxic relational strategies that we were subject to as well as ones we have subjected others to. Paying attention to the bidirectional flow of these patterns is the first step in true change.

This list is based on research and training materials from multiple sources including the Safer Society Foundation, the University of Iowa, Moral Reconation Therapy, and my office partner (work wife) Brenda Martinez, who is a trauma-informed licensed professional counselor and licensed sex offender treatment provider. It is not intended to represent the totality of toxic relational patterns, but to start a conversation on how they affect your own life.

Anger as Means of Control: When we use anger to control and manipulate the behavior of others. The difference between this kind of anger and impulsive anger is that the anger response is turned off the minute we get what we want.

Authoritarian Dominance: When we hold rigid boundaries and expectations that things be done "our" way.

Belittling: When we treat others (or their feelings, concerns, point of view) as comparatively unimportant.

Black and White Decreeing: When we term everything in extremes. ("I can never trust women," or "All men are players.")

Blaming: When we place blame elsewhere or insist that others are responsible for our behavior. Also could be termed a refusal to accept responsibility.

Compartmentalization of Behavior: When we compartmentalize our behavior to keep from feeling guilty, to justify our actions, or to minimize the seriousness of them. ("I only cheat when out of town for work, never when I'm home.")

Credit Seeking: When we want credit for good behavior (Ok, I forgot to pay the electric bill and the power was turned off, but don't I get credit for paying the water bill and the Netflix?) or credit for extremes not engaged in (Ok, I wrecked your car . . . but I could have lied about it and said someone rammed into it while I was at the grocery store), rather than accepting accountability for behavior in question.

Criminal Pride: Feeling a sense of identity and accomplishment from hurting others, e.g. "This is just how I am" or "This is just how I grew up."

Diverting: When we change the subject to something more comfortable, intentionally redirect the conversation, bring up another problem, or intentionally miss the point of the conversation at hand.

Entitlement: When we think someone owes us something or the world owes us something because we are special, different, or have been through more than others have.

Fact Stacking: When we arrange facts in a way to explain our behavior, while omitting other facts that don't work in our favor.

Fairness Violation: When we believe that everyone is treating us unfairly and/or when we keep a mental scorecard regarding "fairness" in the relationship.

Fight Instigating: When we encourage others to fight, then we stand back and watch.

Frequency Minimization: When we minimize the behavior based on frequency. (It didn't happen five times, it was three times at most!). This is a form of playing defense attorney.

Gaslighting: When we deliberately obscure or twist facts to make others question their reality, memory, and ultimate sanity.

Grandiosity: When we make little things into huge, important things so we can shift the focus of attention.

Harm Discounting: When we insist that our actions did not cause the level of harm that others say they did. ("I did it, but it is certainly not as bad as you think.") This is another form of playing defense attorney.

Helplessness: When we act incapable or helpless and unable to do things for ourselves, needing others to do them for us.

Impulsiveness: When we can't wait for what we want and do not want to delay our desires and pursue these desires at the expense of others.

Intention Denial: When we deny our intention for harm. It may be true that we didn't intend to be hurtful or didn't plan a way to control someone else, but that doesn't lessen the impact of our behavior and it is another way of diminishing our responsibility for our actions. ("I didn't mean it" or "Things just got out of control.")

Justice Seeking: When we punish or control others and frame it as punitive toward others because of their behavior toward us. This is another form of playing defense attorney.

Justifying: When we justify our behavior so we don't have to take responsibility ("I wouldn't have hit you if you hadn't made me so angry).

Keeping Score: When we explain or justify behavior based on the past actions of others or ourselves. ("I've always done more than you, so it's not a big deal that I didn't do what I said I would this week.")

Lying: When we intentionally state things that are not true, or do not include all details in an attempt to deceive.

Making Excuses: Similar to justifying, in that we use it to explain away our behavior rather than hold ourselves accountable. ("I was depressed that day.")

Making Fools of: When we exaggerate the mistakes and weaknesses of others to intentionally demean them and lessen their voice and authority.

Minimizing: When we try to make a behavior seem like it has less impact on those around us. ("At least I only made out with them and didn't sleep with them.")

Mind Reading: When we think we know what other people are thinking and make decisions based on these assumptions, rather than asking.

Ownership: When we feel a sense of ownership of other people, and feel entitled to control their behavior.

Phoniness: When we communicate and apologize insincerely, without fully taking responsibility and without intent to change (maybe just intending to stop getting caught).

Playing Dumb: When we act confused about a situation to avoid responsibility for our behavior, or continuously ask questions that imply we don't understand what others are communicating. ("What did I do? What's wrong with that? What do you mean by that?")

Projecting: When we presume what others are thinking, feeling, or doing based on what we are thinking, feeling, or doing.

Pushing Buttons: When we intentionally use information about another person to get them upset in order to distract from our behavior.

Secretive Behavior: When we hide our activities and omit information to keep people from knowing what we are doing.

Selfish Intent: When we think and act in terms of our needs only, and not the needs of others.

Self-Pitying: When we use statements decrying how bad we are in order to get attention paid to us. ("No one cares about me" or "Everyone would be better off without me around.")

Spiritual/Philosophical Bypassing: When we invoke religion or spirituality over personal responsibility in an attempt to ascribe different meaning to a situation or to avoid doing the work around uncomfortable emotions. ("I'm just turning it over to God" or "What does any of this mean at a constructivist level, anyway?")

Uniqueness: When we believe that we are unique in such a way that consideration of others (and sometimes rules and laws regarding conduct) do not apply to us in the same way.

Vagueness: When we respond vaguely or unclearly in order to distract from the truth or the content of the conversation.

Victimization Reversal: When we present ourselves as the victim in a scenario, rather than taking responsibility for our role in any events that occurred.

Wearing Down: When we continuously challenge others to give us what we want until they acquiesce out of exhaustion over the continued fighting.

Zero State: Feeling worthless, like nothing, like a no-body, and/or empty inside and behaving in ways to help fill that void. This is often where narcissistic behavior stems from.

Questions to consider as you go through this list:

- Did you notice any patterns in your answers? Do certain strategies come up time and again?

- What strategies have you used on other people?

- Do you use different strategies for different people (partners vs. friends vs. family, for example)?

- What strategies were used against you in the past? By whom?

- What strategies are being used against you in current relationships? By whom?

- Are there any patterns that you notice in the strategies you use and the ones used against you?

- Are there any patterns that you notice in the strategies that have been used against you in the past and are being used against you in current relationships?

- What is one strategy that you have noticed in yourself that you want to commit to changing? How will you do so?

- What is one strategy that you have noticed in your current relationships that you are committed to no longer accepting? How will you do so?

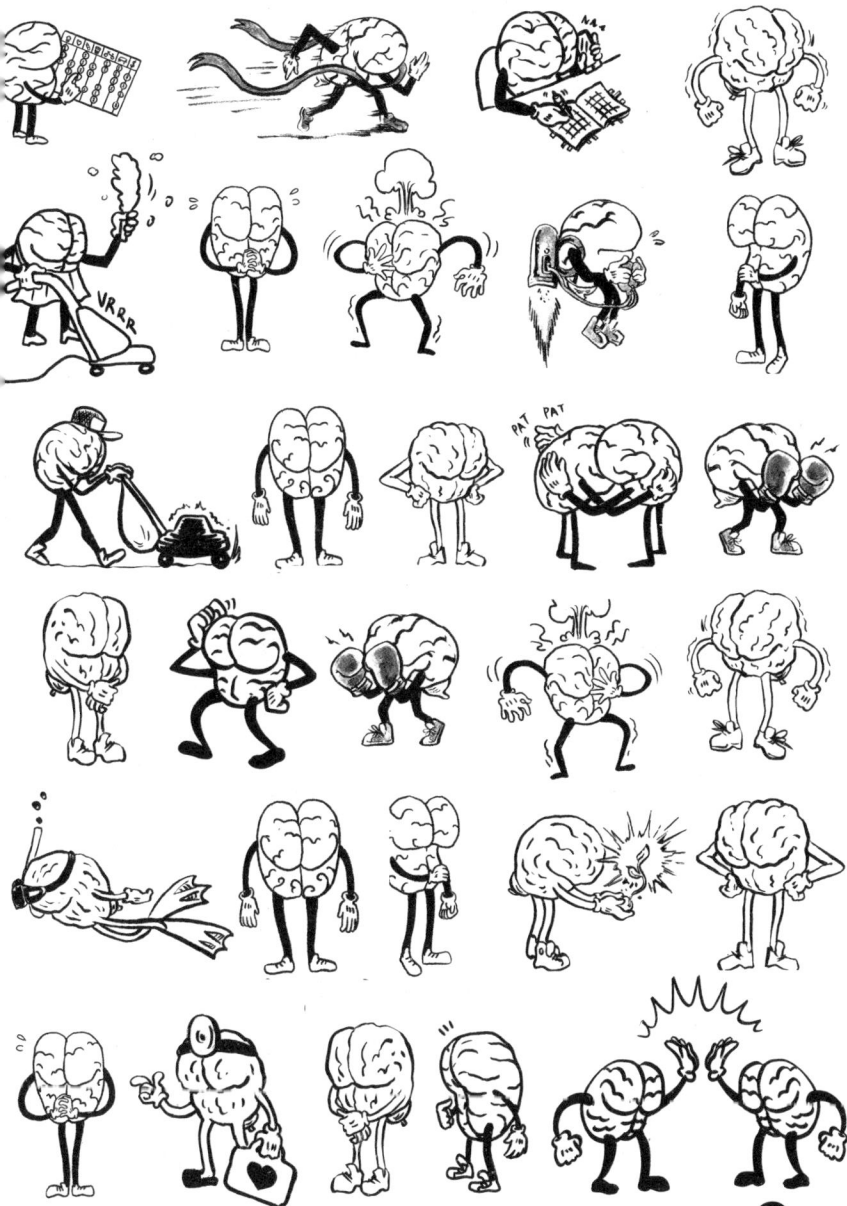

ABOUT THE AUTHOR

Dr. Faith G. Harper, ACS, ACN, is a badass, funny lady with a PhD. She's a licensed professional counselor, board supervisor, certified sexologist, and applied clinical nutritionist with a private practice and consulting business in San Antonio, TX. She has been an adjunct professor and a TEDx presenter, and proudly identifies as a woman of color and uppity intersectional feminist. She is the author of dozens of books.

MORE BY DR. FAITH

Books

The Autism Partner Handbook (with Joe Biel and Elly Blue)

The Autism Relationships Handbook (with Joe Biel)

Befriend Your Brain

Coping Skills

How to Be Accountable (with Joe Biel)

This Is Your Brain on Depression

Unfuck Your Addiction

Unfuck Your Adulting

Unfuck Your Anger

Unfuck Your Anxiety

Unfuck Your Blow Jobs

Unfuck Your Body

Unfuck Your Boundaries

Unfuck Your Brain

Unfuck Your Cunnilingus

Unfuck Your Friendships

Unfuck Your Grief

Unfuck Your Intimacy

Unfuck Your Stress

Unfuck Your Worth

Unfuck Your Writing (with Joe Biel)

Woke Parenting (with Bonnie Scott)

Workbooks

Achieve Your Goals

The Autism Relationships Workbook (with Joe Biel)

How to Be Accountable Workbook (with Joe Biel)

Unfuck Your Anger Workbook

Unfuck Your Anxiety Workbook

Unfuck Your Body Workbook

Unfuck Your Boundaries Workbook

Unfuck Your Intimacy Workbook

Unfuck Your Worth Workbook

Unfuck Your Year

Zines

The Autism Handbook (with Joe Biel)

BDSM FAQ

Dating

Defriending

Detox Your Masculinity (with Aaron Sapp)

Emotional Freedom Technique

Getting Over It

How to Find a Therapist

How to Say No

Indigenous Noms

Relationshipping

The Revolution Won't Forget the Holidays

Self-Compassion

Sex Tools

Sexing Yourself

STI FAQ (with Aaron Sapp)

Surviving

This Is Your Brain on Addiction

This Is Your Brain on Grief

This Is Your Brain on PTSD

Unfuck Your Consent

Unfuck Your Forgiveness

Unfuck Your Mental Health Paradigm

Unfuck Your Sleep

Unfuck Your Work

Vision Boarding

Woke Parenting #1–6 (with Bonnie Scott)

Other

Boundaries Conversation Deck

Stress Coping Skills Deck

How Do You Feel Today? (poster)